Fundamentals of Trace and Log Analysis

A Pattern-Oriented Approach to Monitoring, Diagnostics, and Debugging

Dmitry Vostokov

Apress®

Fundamentals of Trace and Log Analysis: A Pattern-Oriented Approach to Monitoring, Diagnostics, and Debugging

Dmitry Vostokov
Dalkey, Dublin, Ireland

ISBN-13 (pbk): 978-1-4842-9895-4   ISBN-13 (electronic): 978-1-4842-9896-1
https://doi.org/10.1007/978-1-4842-9896-1

Managing Director, Apress Media LLC: Welmoed Spahr
Acquisitions Editor: Celestin Suresh John
Development Editor: James Markham
Editorial Assistant: Gryffin Winkler

Cover designed by eStudioCalamar

Cover image by Jason Leung on Unsplash (www.unsplash.com)

Distributed to the book trade worldwide by Springer Science+Business Media New York, 1 New York Plaza, Suite 4600, New York, NY 10004-1562, USA. Phone 1-800-SPRINGER, fax (201) 348-4505, e-mail orders-ny@springer-sbm.com, or visit www.springeronline.com. Apress Media, LLC is a California LLC and the sole member (owner) is Springer Science + Business Media Finance Inc (SSBM Finance Inc). SSBM Finance Inc is a **Delaware** corporation.

For information on translations, please e-mail booktranslations@springernature.com; for reprint, paperback, or audio rights, please e-mail bookpermissions@springernature.com.

Apress titles may be purchased in bulk for academic, corporate, or promotional use. eBook versions and licenses are also available for most titles. For more information, reference our Print and eBook Bulk Sales web page at http://www.apress.com/bulk-sales.

Any source code or other supplementary material referenced by the author in this book is available to readers on GitHub (github.com/apress). For more detailed information, please visit https://www.apress.com/gp/services/source-code.

Paper in this product is recyclable

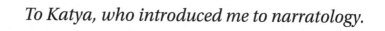

To Katya, who introduced me to narratology.

Table of Contents

About the Author

Dmitry Vostokov is an internationally recognized expert, speaker, educator, scientist, inventor, and author. He founded the pattern-oriented software diagnostics, forensics, and prognostics discipline (Systematic Software Diagnostics) and Software Diagnostics Institute (DA+TA: DumpAnalysis.org + TraceAnalysis.org). Vostokov has also authored multiple books on software diagnostics, anomaly detection and analysis, software and memory forensics, root cause analysis and problem solving, memory dump analysis, debugging, software trace and log analysis, reverse engineering, and malware analysis. He has over 30 years of experience in software architecture, design, development, and maintenance in various industries, including leadership, technical, and people management roles. In his spare time, he presents multiple topics on Debugging.TV and explores Software Narratology and its further development as Narratology of Things and Diagnostics of Things (DoT), Software Pathology, and Quantum Software Diagnostics. His current interest areas are theoretical software diagnostics and its mathematical and computer science foundations, application of formal logic, artificial intelligence, machine learning, and data mining to diagnostics and anomaly detection, software diagnostics engineering and diagnostics-driven development, diagnostics workflow, and interaction. Recent interest areas also include cloud-native computing, security, automation, functional programming, applications of category theory to software development and big data, and artificial intelligence diagnostics.

About the Technical Reviewer

Vijender Singh, a multicloud professional with over six years of expertise, holds an MSc with distinction from Liverpool John Moores University, where his research centered on keyphrase extraction. He boasts an impressive collection of certifications, including MLPE GCP, five Azure certifications, two AWS certifications, and TensorFlow certification. Vijender's role as a technical reviewer for numerous books reflects his commitment to improving the future.

LinkedIn: www.linkedin.com/in/vijendersingh412

Introduction

This book will help you analyze traces and logs from different software environments and communicate analysis results using a pattern language that covers everything from a small debugging log to a distributed trace with billions of messages from hundreds of computers, thousands of software components, threads, and processes.

The book begins with the basic terminology of operating systems and programming, the foundation for understanding trace and log analysis. It then talks about patterns that help describe problems from a user's view and patterns for errors and failures. Then, the book covers a range of trace patterns that group messages and explores how logs depict software activities. It even looks at specific message patterns and how they connect in a single trace. Toward the end, the book goes over patterns for multiple traces and logs and how to understand them as data. In this way, you can use similar methods to find problems across a wide variety of software. It also guides you on analyzing issues on systems such as Windows, macOS, Linux, Android, iOS, and other types of computers, including those in networks and the Internet of Things, regardless of their system differences.

Upon completing this book, you will be able to navigate the complexities of trace and log analysis and apply uniform diagnostics and anomaly detection pattern language across diverse software environments to help you troubleshoot, debug, and fix issues.

The book will be useful for software technical support engineers, system and network administrators, software developers, testers, DevOps and DevSecOps, digital forensics and malware analysts, security incident response engineers, data analysts, and data mining practitioners.

CHAPTER 1

Introduction

We start this chapter with a few words about the need for this book. Almost 20 years ago, I started doing Windows software diagnostics full time as a member of the technical support and escalation team at a large global software vendor. In addition to crash and hang dump analysis, the job required analysis of software traces similar to that of *Process Monitor*[1] log format with messages from hundreds of processes and thousands of threads totaling millions of lines (Figure 1-1). Gradually I became aware that we need a similar pattern-driven system as I devised for memory dump analysis.[2] However, after a few patterns, such as **Periodic Error**, I was stuck devising more. At this time, through my voracious independent reading, I accidentally became acquainted with narratology,[3] a discipline that studies narration and narrative stories. So this became the foundation for what I later named Software Narratology, a new approach to the study of software narrative, stories of computation. Viewing software traces as narratives helped devise general analysis patterns to structure trace and log analysis independent of OS and products. Although this book teaches some analysis patterns in a Windows context, you can apply them to your specific environment and product domain problems. Some examples are

---

[1] https://learn.microsoft.com/en-gb/sysinternals/downloads/procmon

[2] Dmitry Vostokov, Encyclopedia of Crash Dump Analysis Patterns: Detecting Abnormal Software Structure and Behavior in Computer Memory, Third Edition, 2020 (ISBN-13: 978-1912636303)

[3] https://en.wikipedia.org/wiki/Narratology

© Dmitry Vostokov 2023
D. Vostokov, *Fundamentals of Trace and Log Analysis*,
https://doi.org/10.1007/978-1-4842-9896-1_1

illustrated with Process Monitor and Event Tracing for Windows[4] because they are widely used and not tied to specific products. In addition to native logging, Linux has LTTng[5] tracing. All these tracing frameworks produce trace and log files with conceptually similar formats.

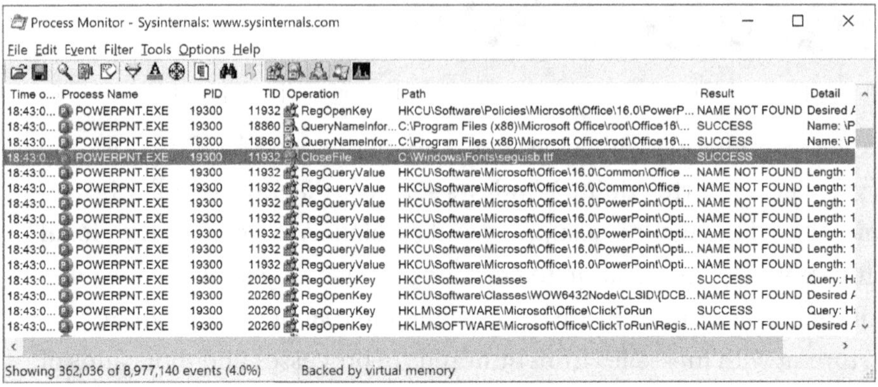

Figure 1-1. *A Process Monitor log example*

First, we review the essential fundamentals necessary for software trace and log analysis. Then we learn about software trace analysis patterns that were classified into several categories. We cover more than 60 basic analysis patterns. Additional patterns can be found in the frequently updated reference.[6] One note: this book is about software trace and log analysis and not about software trace implementation, internals, and collection methods and tools.

The basic concepts we review in this chapter include processes, threads, components (or modules), source code files, source code or API functions, and stack traces (or backtraces). One additional concept stays

---

[4] https://learn.microsoft.com/en-us/windows/win32/etw/about-event-tracing

[5] https://lttng.org/

[6] Dmitry Vostokov, Trace, Log, Text, Narrative, Data: An Analysis Pattern Reference for Information Mining, Diagnostics, Anomaly Detection, Fifth Edition, 2023 (ISBN-13: 978-1912636587)

out. It is called **Adjoint Thread**, and we introduce and discuss it after we review threads. Together with threads, adjoint threads are absolutely essential for software trace analysis.

Software Trace/Log

What is a software trace or log, actually? For our purposes, it is just a sequence of formatted messages sent from running software. They are usually arranged by time and can be considered as a software narrative story (Figure 1-2). In this training, we confine ourselves to the analysis of such logs and what patterns to look for.

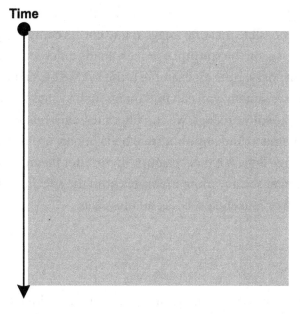

Figure 1-2. A software trace or log in the most general form

3

Process

An operating system process is a container for resources such as memory, files, and synchronization objects. Even the OS kernel itself can be considered a process itself (in Windows, it is usually called just System). Each process has its own process identifier, PID (process ID). In Windows, it belongs to a user session; for example, there can be several users logged into Windows. Each process has its own image name, such as `notepad.exe`, and a list of associated loaded DLL (dynamic-link library) modules (or shared libraries in Linux/macOS). An image name is also a module. It is important to remember that there can be several processes running, each having the same image name, for example, two instances of `notepad.exe`. The list of DLLs in both instances, most of the time, is identical. At the same time, it is possible that one image name covers completely different processes because, on the startup, a process loads different modules for different purposes. Here an example is the `svchost` executable. On a running Windows system, you can find many such `svchost` processes. When we analyze software logs, we can filter messages related to a specific PID or image name to find any abnormal behavior according to the expected message flow. A typical example here: after the middle of the full trace, we no longer see any more messages from the specific PID, not even any termination or graceful process end messages.

Thread

In Windows and macOS, a thread is an execution unit with its own ID and is owned by some process, for example, `calculator.exe`. In Linux, threads are almost the same as processes but share the same virtual memory. Remember that trace messages come from some thread because we need to execute some code to emit a trace message. Each thread is executed on some CPU and, in general, can have its CPU changed during execution history. Filtering by threads, for example, allows us to find any anomalous behavior, such as blocked execution activity and various execution delays. In Figure 1-3, we see a discontinuity for TID 2 and a delay in TID 1.

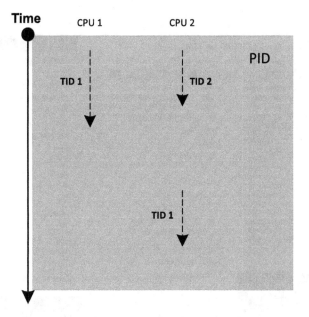

Figure 1-3. *An illustration of different threads*

Adjoint Thread

If a thread is a linear ordered flow of activities associated with a particular TID (thread ID), as seen from a trace message perspective through time, we can also extend this flow concept and consider a linear flow of activities associated with some other parameter such as PID, CPU, or message text. Such messages have different TIDs associated with them but have some chosen constant parameter or column value in a trace viewing tool. The name **adjoint** comes from the fact that in threads of activity, TID stays the same, but other message attributes vary; in adjoint threads, we have the opposite. In Windows Process Monitor, we use exclusive and inclusive filtering to form adjoint threads. By applying complex filtering criteria, we get **Adjoint Threads** from other adjoint threads, for example, an adjoint thread with specific PID and file activity formed after an inspection of an adjoint thread with the same image name, such as POWERPNT.EXE (Figure 1-4).

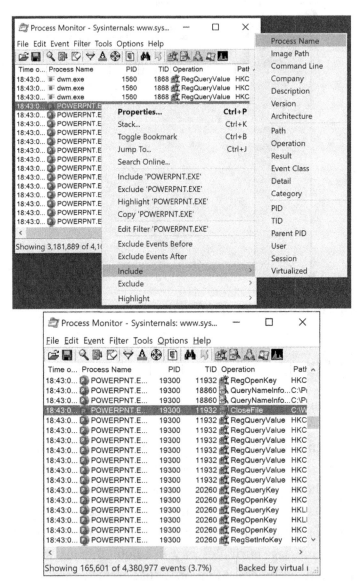

Figure 1-4. *An illustration of Adjoint Thread using Process Monitor*

Component/Module/Source

Trace messages come from a thread that belongs to a PID, but the code to emit them resides in source code files. Some source code files, such as static library code, can also be reused and included in different modules (Figure 1-5). Such DLL modules or shared libraries can also be loaded into different processes. Therefore, source or module (in a simpler) case is another grouping of messages based on subsystem and functional division that may include several source code files. By module or source filtering, we can see subsystem activities.

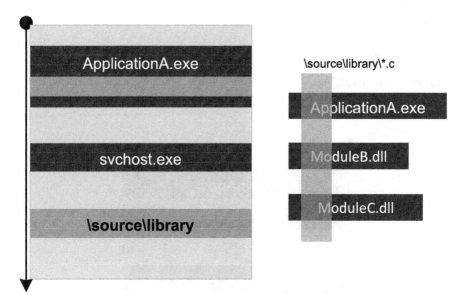

Figure 1-5. *An illustration of the same source code used in different modules*

File and Function

Source code consists of files, and each file has some functions inside that do the actual tracing. With a file or function filtering (selecting only messages that belong to particular files or functions), we can see the flow of certain functionality that is more fine-grained than the source or module **Adjoint Thread of Activity** (Listing 1-1 and Figure 1-6).

Listing 1-1. An example of file and function

```
// MainApp.c
foo () {
  trace("foo: entry");
  // do stuff
  trace("foo: exit");
}
```

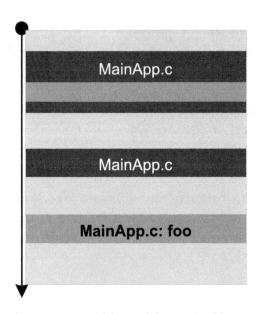

Figure 1-6. *An illustration of file and function filtering*

Trace Message

A formatted trace message is just a sentence with some invariant and variable parts (Listing 1-2 and Figure 1-7). In fact, it is possible to trace invariant and variable parts, the so-called **Message Invariant** and **Data Flow** analysis patterns that we consider later.

Listing 1-2. Trace message examples

```
foo () {
  trace("foo: entry");
  int result = bar();
  trace("bar result: 555");
  trace("foo: exit");
}
```

Invariant	*Variable*	Invariant	*Variable*	...

Figure 1-7. *A general trace message format*

Stack Trace

Because each trace message originated from some function in the source code, it has an associated stack trace similar to a live debugging scenario where we put a breakpoint at a trace message code location (Listing 1-3 and Figure 1-8). Usually, stack traces (or backtraces) are read from bottom to top, as in a debugger, but some execution environments prefer to generate them the other way around, for example, Python's tracebacks.[7]

---

[7] Dmitry Vostokov, Python Debugging for AI, Machine Learning, and Cloud Computing: A Pattern-Oriented Approach, 2023 (ISBN-13: 978-1484297445)

Listing 1-3. An example source code with tracing

```
main() {
  trace("start");
  foo();
}

foo() {
  trace("foo: entry");
  bar();
}

bar() {
  trace("bar: entry");
  // do stuff
}
```

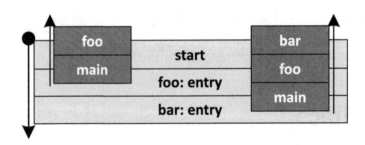

Figure 1-8. An execution trace with corresponding stack trace

Minimal Trace Graphs

In order to illustrate trace analysis patterns graphically, we use the simplified abstract pictorial representation of a typical software trace (Figure 1-9). It has all essential features such as message number, time, PID, TID, and message text itself. Sometimes, for illustration purposes, I also provide trace fragments in a textual form where I include or exclude certain message attributes (or columns) such as message source or module, time, or date (Listing 1-4).

Listing 1-4. A sample trace fragment

```
No Module  PID  TID  Date       Time         Message
--------------------------------------------------------------
1  ModuleA 4280 1736 01/01/2023 08:53:50.496 Trace message 1
2  ModuleB 6212 6216 01/01/2023 08:53:52.876 Trace message 2
...
```

Figure 1-9. A typical trace graph

Pattern-Oriented Analysis

A few definitions related to patterns: software trace analysis is usually an analysis of a text for the presence of patterns using analysis patterns. The distinction between patterns, analysis patterns, and pattern languages is summarized in the following definitions.

- **Diagnostic Pattern**: A common recurrent identifiable problem together with a set of recommendations and possible solutions to apply in a specific context

- **Diagnostic Problem**: A set of indicators (symptoms, signs) describing a problem

- **Diagnostic Analysis Pattern**: A common recurrent analysis technique and method of diagnostic pattern identification in a specific context

- **Diagnostics Pattern Language**: Common names of diagnostic and diagnostic analysis patterns; the same language for any operating system: Windows, macOS, Linux

Pattern catalogs are rarely fixed. New patterns are constantly discerned, especially at a domain-specific level, such as product- and platform-specific patterns. New analysis patterns are also devised when new techniques are discovered or borrowed from other knowledge domains.

Pattern-driven and pattern-based approaches (together with systemic knowledge transfer) form pattern-oriented trace and log analysis.

The analysis patterns we discuss in this book are general and domain-independent and can be applied to analyze different software logs, from IBM mainframes to cloud native to mobile and embedded computers. The next level is domain-specific patterns, such as product or OS error messages (Figure 1-10). Of course, to get most of the patterns, you need to know your specific problem domain. An analogy would be a story about some country where you don't know anything about its history or the meaning of events and places, but you still can recognize the general story structure; for example, a person was waiting for two hours to get an audience. From your past experience, you know that every audience has a queue.

Pattern Classification

Analysis patterns may be classified into several categories. The **Vocabulary** category consists of patterns related to a problem description. The **Error** category covers general error distribution patterns. We also consider **Traces as Wholes**, their **Large-Scale** structure, **Activity** patterns, patterns related to individual trace **Message** structure, patterns related to collections of messages (the so-called **Blocks**), patterns related to several traces and logs as a collection of artifacts from software incident (**Trace Set**), and finally, **Data** patterns related to treating traces and logs as data. We discuss all these categories in the coming chapters in detail.

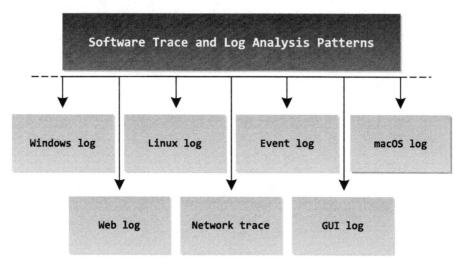

Figure 1-10. *Domain pattern hierarchy*

Summary

In this first chapter, we introduced basic concepts related to software traces and logs and their analysis with graphical illustrations. The next chapters introduce different pattern categories and we start with **Vocabulary** patterns.

CHAPTER 2

Vocabulary Patterns

The first block of patterns we cover is **Vocabulary patterns**. These are patterns related to problem description from a user's point of view. Their pattern language names are

- Basic Facts
- Vocabulary Index

Basic Facts

A typical trace is a detailed software narrative that may include lots of irrelevant information with useful messages like needles in a haystack. However, it is usually accompanied by a problem description that lists essential facts, for example, *"Application disappears after launch."* Or we hope it lists essential facts. Therefore, the first task of any trace analysis is to check the presence of **Basic Facts** (or it is usually called Supporting Materials) in the trace (Listing 2-1). If they are not visible or do not correspond, then the trace was possibly not recorded during the problem or was taken from a different computer or under different conditions. Here is a negative example: An application disappears after launch. We look at the trace and find several application launches. Which one to look for? What if they all disappear suddenly because the tracing ends before

© Dmitry Vostokov 2023
D. Vostokov, *Fundamentals of Trace and Log Analysis,*
https://doi.org/10.1007/978-1-4842-9896-1_2

they finish? We see how vital basic facts are. Is it still possible to diagnose which one disappeared? Sometimes it is possible, and for example, here, it might be a discontinuity, the disappearance of all messages related to that application PID till the end of the trace compared with other applications' messages that populate the trace till the end unless the application finishes correctly. Here we can use the so-called **Adjoint Thread** pattern to filter trace messages for specific PID and compare their **Partition** and **Characteristic Message Blocks** (other patterns) and search for error patterns and any **Guest Components** (the latter is suddenly appearing trace messages from a loaded module that we never see loaded in normal working scenarios).

Listing 2-1. An example software trace related to a problem description

```
PID     Message
-----------------------------------
...
3f6     Create process AppA: PID 4a5
4a5     AppA loads DLLC
...
3f6     Create process AppB: PID 5b8
5b8     AppB loads DLLD
...
```

Related patterns are

- Vocabulary Index

Basic Facts Taxonomy

We propose the following taxonomy of **Basic Facts**:

- **Functional Facts**: For example, expected a dialog to enter data

- **Nonfunctional Facts**: For example, CPU consumption 100%

- **Identification Facts**: For example, application name, PID, username

Software is written according to some requirements, such as functional ones, such as what it is supposed to do and what users are expected to see and get during the interaction, and nonfunctional ones, such as a requirement that software execution should not exceed resource usage. Deviations from such requirements map to facts in software problem descriptions. The third type of facts is problem instance-specific such as a username or PID that helps to identify specific software interaction in the software execution story. For example, suppose you analyze a user session problem from a multiuser server environment. You get a software trace or log with a hundred users, and you need a username to search for and problem process PID to filter its threads.

Vocabulary Index

What will we do when confronted with 10 million trace messages recorded during an hour with an average trace **Message Current** of 3,000 msg/s from dozens of modules and having a short problem description even if it has some basic facts? One solution is to search for a specific

17

vocabulary relevant to the problem description; for example, if a problem is an authentication failure, we might try to search for words related to authentication (Figure 2-1). We call such a list of words drawn from the troubleshooting domain **Vocabulary Index** by analogy with book index. In our trace example, the search for "authentication" jumps straight to a smaller **Activity Region** (another pattern) of authentication modules starting from message #1,380,010. The last "password" occurrence is in message #3,380,490, which narrows the initial analysis region to just 500 messages (Figure 2-2).

Figure 2-1. *A problem description example*

Related patterns are

- Basic Facts

- Activity Region

Figure 2-2. *An illustration of the narrowing of the analysis region*

Summary

In this chapter, we introduced the basic trace and log analysis patterns from the **Vocabulary** category. The next chapter introduces **Error** patterns.

## CHAPTER 3

Error Patterns

The next block of patterns we cover is **Error Patterns**. These patterns are related to error and failure messages, either explicitly stating that there is an error or doing that indirectly via error code, abnormal function return value, or (in the case of Windows systems) NT status value in the failure range. Their pattern language names are

- Error Message

- Exception Stack Trace

- False Positive Error

- Periodic Error ↓[1]

- Error Distribution

Error Message

This **Error Message** can be reported either explicitly ("operation failed") or implicitly as an operation status value, such as 0xC00000XX, or a value different from a normal result, such as when we get 5 instead of 0. Some debuggers, for example, WinDbg, have a special command to show a textual description of an error or status value (Listing 3-1). It is considered a good implementation practice to indicate in trace messages

---

[1] "↓" sign means that a pattern involves time dependency.

whether a number value was supplied for information only and should be ignored by technical support or software maintenance engineers. Some error messages may contain information irrelevant to the current software incident, the so-called **False Positive Errors** (another pattern we discuss later). Some tracing architectures and tools include the message information category for errors and warnings (e.g., severity level), where you can filter by error category to get the **Adjoint Thread** of errors. Note that the association of a trace statement with an error category is left at the discretion of a software engineer writing code, and you can have error messages that do not belong to the error category. Errors you find or are interested in can be repeated throughout the log (**Periodic Error** pattern); they can also be unevenly distributed throughout the trace or log (**Error Distribution** pattern) and, if filtered by their data value, can show these errors **Data Flow** across threads, processes, and modules.

Listing 3-1. WinDbg !error debugger extension command example

```
0:000> !error c0000017
Error code: (NTSTATUS) 0xc0000017 (3221225495) - {Not Enough
Quota}  Not enough virtual memory or paging file quota is
available to complete the specified operation.
```

```
0:000> !error 5
Error code: (Win32) 0x5 (5) - Access is denied.
```

Related patterns are

- False Positive Error

- Periodic Error

- Error Distribution

- Adjoint Thread

- Data Flow

Exception Stack Trace

Often analysis of software traces starts with searching for short textual patterns, like a failure, an exception code, or simply the word "exception." And indeed, some software components are able to record their own exceptions or exceptions that were propagated to them, including full stack traces. This behavior is all common in .NET and Java environments. Listing 3-2 shows a typical example based on real software traces. These **Exception Stack Traces** are similar to stack traces we see in memory dumps. In the embedded stack trace, we see that the App object was trying to enumerate business objects and asked the Store object to get some data, and the latter object was probably trying to communicate with the real data store via DCOM.

Listing 3-2. Exception Stack Trace pattern example

```
No      PID  TID  Message
------------------------

...

265799 8984 4216 ComponentA.Store.GetData threw exception:
'System.Reflection.TargetInvocationException: DCOM connection to
server failed with error: 'Exception from HRESULT: 0x842D0001' ->
System.Runtime.InteropServices.COMException (0x842D0001):
Exception from HRESULT: 0x842D0001
265800 8984 4216 === Exception Stack Trace ===
265801 8984 4216 at System.Runtime.Remoting.Proxies.RealProxy.
HandleReturnMessage(IMessage reqMsg, IMessage retMsg)
265802 8984 4216 at System.Runtime.Remoting.Proxies.RealProxy.
PrivateInvoke(MessageData& msgData, Int32 type)
265803 8984 4216 at ComponentA.Store.GetData(Byte[] pKey)
265804 8984 4216 at ComponentA.App.EnumBusinessObjects()
...
```

Related patterns are

- Error Message

Periodic Error

Periodic Error is an **Error Message** observed periodically many times in a trace or log file (Figure 3-1). In fact, it may not be exactly the same trace message. It may differ in some reported values having the same **Message Invariant** structure (another message-level pattern).

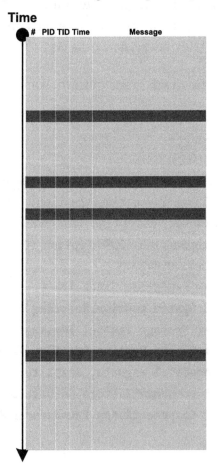

Figure 3-1. *An illustration of* ***Periodic Error*** *pattern*

Related patterns are

- Error Message

- Error Distribution

- False Positive Error

- Message Invariant

False Positive Error

The software might report errors that are false positive, irrelevant to the reported problem, or expected as a part of an implementation detail, for example, when a function returns an error to indicate that a bigger buffer is required or to estimate its size for a subsequent call. To know if some error message is False **Positive Error** or not, we compare the same **Activity Regions** in a trace from the problem scenario to a trace from the normal working scenario or the so-called **Master Trace**.

Related patterns are

- Error Message

- Master Trace

- Activity Region

Error Distribution

Sometimes we need to pay attention to **Error Distribution**, for example, the distribution of the same error across a software log space or different error messages in different parts of the same software log or trace (providing effective **Partition** of the trace into error **Activity Regions**, Figure 3-2).

Related patterns are

- Partition
- Activity Region

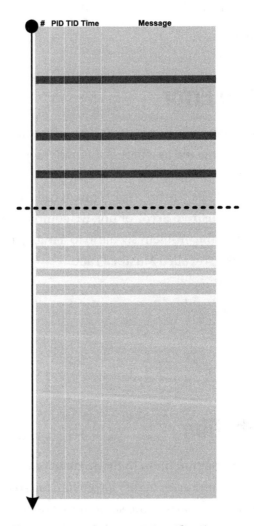

Figure 3-2. *An illustration of **Error Distribution** pattern*

Summary

In this chapter, we introduced the basic trace and log analysis patterns from the **Error** category. The next chapter introduces **Trace as a Whole** patterns.

CHAPTER 4

Trace As a Whole

The third block of patterns we cover is related to the software **Trace as a Whole**. Here we ignore trace or log message contents and treat all messages statistically. Their pattern language names are

- Partition
- Circular Trace ↓
- Message Density
- Message Current ↓
- Trace Acceleration ↓
- No Trace Metafile
- Empty Trace
- Missing Component
- Guest Component
- Truncated Trace ↓
- Visibility Limit
- Sparse Trace

© Dmitry Vostokov 2023
D. Vostokov, *Fundamentals of Trace and Log Analysis,*
https://doi.org/10.1007/978-1-4842-9896-1_4

Partition

Here we introduce a software narratological (like a software story) **Partitioning** of a trace into Head, Prologue, Core, Epilogue, and Tail segments (Figure 4-1). Some elements, such as Head and Tail, may be optional and combined with Prologue and Epilogue. This pattern is useful for comparative software trace analysis. For example, suppose a trace started just before the problem reproduction steps or a particular **Significant Event** and finished just after the last reproduction steps or after another **Significant Event**. Then its core trace messages are surrounded by the prologue and epilogue messages. What is before and after are not really needed for analysis (like noise). The size of a core trace segment need not be the same because environments and executed code paths might differ. However, often some traces are **Truncated Traces** (another pattern). Please note that such partitioning can be done for any filtered trace, such as an **Adjoint Thread of Activity**.

Figure 4-1. *An illustration of **Partition** pattern*

Related patterns are

- Significant Event

- Truncated Trace

- Adjoint Thread

Circular Trace

One of the common problems with tracing is rare and non-reproducible incidents. If the amount of tracing messages is small per second, it is possible to record events for hours or days. However, if we need to trace all events to do filtering later, then trace files can grow uncontrollably. Therefore, some tools enable circular tracing, and after reaching a particular file size, the tracing stream overwrites older messages. Such **Circular Traces** can be detected from timestamps, like in Listing 4-1 on this slide. Here the analysis **Focus of Tracing** region is found at the beginning of the trace because as soon as the elusive and hard-to-reproduce problem happened, the tracing was stopped (Figure 4-2).

Listing 4-1. Circular Trace pattern example

```
No      Module  PID  TID  Date      Time         Message
-----------------------------------------------------------------
1       ModuleA 4280 1736 1/1/2023 08:53:50.496 Trace message 1
2       ModuleB 6212 6216 1/1/2023 08:53:52.876 Trace message 2
3       ModuleA 4280 4776 1/1/2023 08:54:13.537 Trace message 3
...
3799    ModuleA 4280 3776 1/1/2023 09:15:00.853 Trace
        message 3799
3800    ModuleA 4280 1736 1/1/2023 09:42:12.029 Trace
        message 3800
...
579210 ModuleA 4280 4776 1/1/2023 08:53:35.989 Trace
message 579210
```

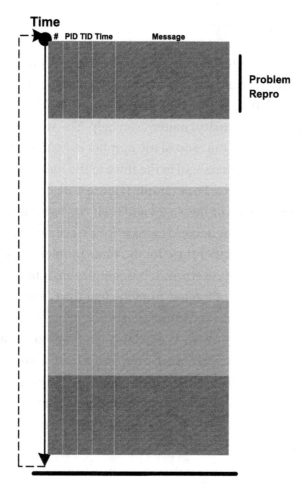

Figure 4-2. An illustration of **Circular Trace** pattern

Related patterns are

- Focus of Tracing

Message Density

Sometimes we have several disjoint **Foci of Tracing** and possible false positives. We wonder where we should start our analysis and assign relative priorities for troubleshooting suggestions. Here **Message Density** (also called **Statement Density**) pattern can help. The statement or message density is simply the ratio of the number of occurrences of the specific trace statement (message) in the trace to the total number of all different recorded messages. For example (Figure 4-3), consider a software trace with two frequent error messages and their corresponding trace densities, D11 and D21. The second index is for a trace number. Suppose their relative ratio is 6. Another trace for the same problem was collected at a different time with the same errors. It has many more total messages and only a few error messages of interest from the first trace. However, the ratio of densities is approximately the same, suggesting that error messages are correlated. For the second trace, density is ten times lower, and this suggests these problems might have started much later, at some time after the start of the trace recording, and a much bigger noise part (head part) from the trace **Partition**. We also look at the **Relative Density** pattern again when we consider trace set patterns, patterns for trace message collections and sets.

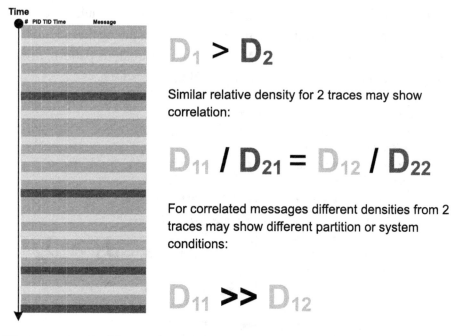

$$D_1 > D_2$$

Similar relative density for 2 traces may show correlation:

$$D_{11} / D_{21} = D_{12} / D_{22}$$

For correlated messages different densities from 2 traces may show different partition or system conditions:

$$D_{11} >> D_{12}$$

Figure 4-3. *An illustration of **Message Density** pattern*

Related patterns are

- Intra-correlation
- Focus of Tracing
- Relative Density
- Partition

Message Current

Message Current (also called **Statement Current**) is the number of messages per unit of time (named as J in Figure 4-4). This pattern is similar to velocity, a first-order derivative. A trace can also be partitioned into **Activity Regions** with different currents, and current can also be measured between significant events such as process start and exit. A high trace current can be an indication of high CPU activity if a spiking thread has trace messages. Together with the **Message Density** analysis pattern, this pattern can help in prioritizing troubleshooting suggestions.

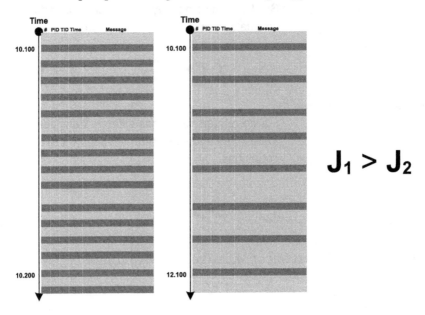

Figure 4-4. *An illustration of **Message Current** pattern*

Related patterns are

- Significant Event

- Activity Region

- Message Density

Trace Acceleration

Sometimes we have a sequence of **Activity Regions** with increasing values of **Message Current** like depicted as J in Figure 4-5. The boundaries of regions may be blurry and arbitrarily drawn, of course. Nevertheless, the current is visibly increasing or decreasing. You can see an analogy with physical acceleration, a second-order derivative. We can also metaphorically use here the notion of a partial derivative for trace **Message Current** and **Trace Acceleration** for **Threads of Activity** and **Adjoint Threads of Activity**.

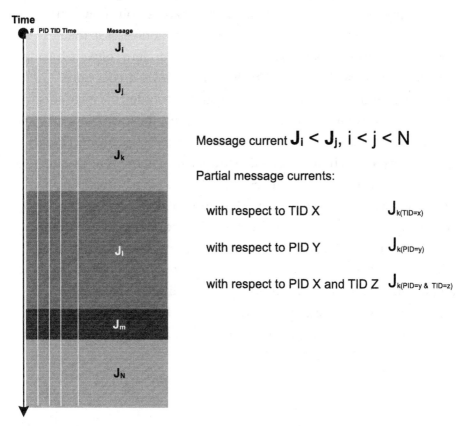

Message current $J_i < J_j$, $i < j < N$

Partial message currents:

with respect to TID X $J_{k(TID=x)}$

with respect to PID Y $J_{k(PID=y)}$

with respect to PID X and TID Z $J_{k(PID=y \ \& \ TID=z)}$

Figure 4-5. *An illustration of* ***Trace Acceleration*** *pattern*

Related patterns are

- Activity Region

- Message Current

- Thread of Activity

- Adjoint Thread of Activity

No Trace Metafile

If you do live debugging and memory dump analysis, you know that symbol files are necessary in order to map binary addresses to their proper symbolic forms, such as function names. Modern software tracing implementations, such as Event Tracing for Windows, do not store message text and formatting information in the recorded message stream. After recording, similar to postmortem debugging, the trace is opened, and associated necessary symbol files are used to convert stored short binary data to an expanded human-readable textual format. In Event Tracing for Windows world, such files are called TMF files (Trace Metafiles). In some cases, when we have **No Trace Metafiles**, it is still possible to detect broad behavioral patterns such as **Circular Trace**, **Message Density** and **Message Current**, **Discontinuity**, **Time Delta**, and **Trace Acceleration**. By looking at **Thread of Activity**, we can also sometimes infer the possible component or module name based on surrounding trace messages with present TMF files, especially when we have source code access. For example, in the trace from Listing 4-2, it can be dllA or any other module that the foo function calls.

Listing 4-2. No Trace Metafile pattern example

```
#      Module  PID   TID  Time          Message
--------------------------------------------
...

21372 dllA     2968 5476 3:55:10.004 Calling foo()
21373 Unknown 2968 5476 3:55:10.004 Unknown
GUID=A1E38F24-613D-4D71-B9F5-… (No Format Information found).
21374 Unknown 2968 5476 3:55:10.004 Unknown
GUID=A1E38F24-613D-4D71-B9F5-… (No Format Information found)
21375 Unknown 2968 5476 3:55:10.004 Unknown
GUID=A1E38F24-613D-4D71-B9F5-… (No Format Information found)
21376 Unknown 2968 5476 3:55:10.004 Unknown
GUID=A1E38F24-613D-4D71-B9F5-… (No Format Information found)
21377 Unknown 2968 5476 3:55:10.004 Unknown
GUID=A1E38F24-613D-4D71-B9F5-… (No Format Information found)
21378 dllA     2968 5476 3:55:10.004 Calling bar()
...
```

Related patterns are

- Thread of Activity

Empty Trace

Empty Trace ranges from a totally empty trace where only a meta trace header (if any) describing the overall trace structure is present to a few messages where we expect thousands. This pattern is also an extreme case of **Truncated Trace**, **No Activity**, and **Missing Component** patterns. Also, please note that an empty trace file doesn't necessarily have a zero file size because a tracing architecture may pre-allocate some file space for block data writing. One important recommendation is to always open a trace before sending it to someone else.

Related patterns are

- Truncated Trace

- No Activity

- Missing Component

Missing Component

Sometimes, we don't see the trace messages we expect and wonder whether a component (module DLL, shared library) was not loaded, its container process ceased to exist, or simply it wasn't selected for tracing (Figure 4-6). In many support cases, there is a trade-off between tracing everything and the size of trace files. Customers and engineers usually prefer smaller files to analyze. However, in the case of predictable and reproducible issues with short duration, we can always select all modules or deselect a few (instead of selecting a few). The **Missing Component** pattern is closely related to the **Discontinuity** pattern with a possibility of a sudden and silent gap in trace statements that could have happened because not all necessary modules or components were selected for tracing. Sometimes, in cases when a component was selected for tracing, but we don't see any trace output from it, other traces from different tracing tools, such as Process Monitor, can give us an indication, for example, showing a load failure message. It is an example of a trace **Inter-correlation** pattern that we cover later.

Figure 4-6. *An illustration of **Missing Component** pattern*

Related patterns are

- Discontinuity

- Inter-correlation

- No Activity

Guest Component

Often, when comparing normal, expected (or working), and abnormal (or nonworking) traces, we can get clues for further troubleshooting and debugging by looking at component (module) load events. For example, when we see an unexpected component load event in our nonworking trace, its function (and sometimes even component name) can signify some differences to pay attention to. The **Guest Component** pattern differs from the **Missing Component** pattern we covered previously. Although in the latter analysis pattern, a missing component in one trace may appear in another trace, the component name is known a priori and expected. In the former pattern, a component is unexpected. For example, in the trace picture earlier, the appearance of `3rdPartyActivity` DLL may suggest further investigation if the activity is related to functional activity in a normal working trace (Figure 4-7). Another example is an OS error reporting component (`WER`, Windows Error Reporting module in Windows).

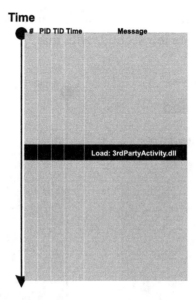

Figure 4-7. *An illustration of **Guest Component** pattern*

Related patterns are

- Missing Component

Truncated Trace

Sometimes a software trace is **Truncated Trace** when a trace session was stopped prematurely, often when a problem didn't manifest itself visually (Figure 4-8). We can diagnose such traces by their short time duration, missing **Anchor Messages**, or **Missing Components** necessary for analysis. My favorite example is user session initialization in a multiuser server environment when problem effects are visible only after the user session is fully initialized and an application is launched. The module that monitors process creation events was included for tracing, and we expect a full-process launch sequence up to an application executable. However, a trace only shows the launch of the user authentication executable and other trace messages for a few seconds after that.

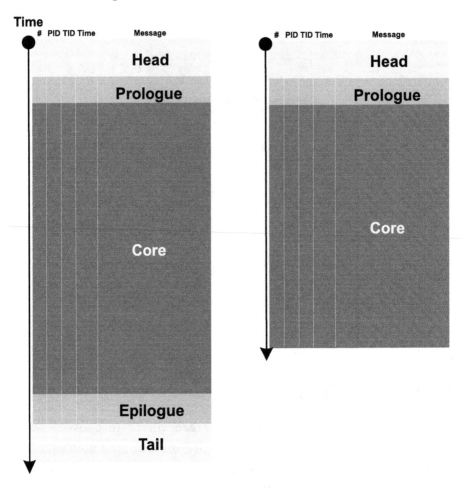

Figure 4-8. *An illustration of **Truncated Trace** pattern*

Related patterns are

- Partition

- Anchor Messages

- Missing Component

Visibility Limit

Sometimes it is not possible to log or trace from the very beginning of a user or system interaction (Figure 4-9). Moreover, internal application tracing cannot trace anything before that application start and its early initialization. The same is for system-wide tracing, which cannot trace before the tracing subsystem or service starts. Therefore, each log has its intrinsic **Visibility Limit** in addition to possible **Truncated Trace** or **Missing Component** patterns that cover cases we can avoid.

Figure 4-9. *An illustration of* ***Visibility Limit*** *pattern*

Related patterns are

- Truncated Trace

- Missing Component

- Sparse Trace

Sparse Trace

Behind any trace statement is a source code fragment (the so-called Program Lines of Trace, or PLOT). This pattern covers the missing trace statements in the source code (Figure 4-10). Potentially it is possible to trace every source code line or implementation language statement, but in practice, trace statements in source code are added only in places when a developer finds it useful to aid possible future debugging. Monitoring tools also trace certain public API and specific functionality such as file and registry access or network communication. Therefore, it is often a case that when we don't see anything in a trace or see very little, this is because a particular source code fragment was not covered by trace statements. This **Sparse Trace** pattern differs from the **Missing Component** pattern, where some components were not explicitly included for tracing, although there is a tracing code there. It also differs from the **Visibility Limit** pattern, where tracing is intrinsically impossible. As a result, after analyzing such traces, technical support and escalation engineers request to add more trace statements, and software engineers extend tracing coverage iteratively as needed.

Related patterns are

- Missing Component

- Visibility Limit

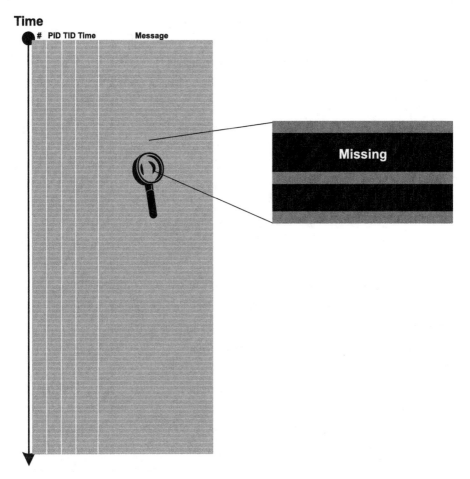

Figure 4-10. *An illustration of **Sparse Trace** pattern*

Summary

In this chapter, we introduced the basic trace and log analysis patterns from the **Trace as a Whole** category. The next chapter introduces **Large-Scale** patterns.

CHAPTER 5

Large-Scale Patterns

The fourth block of analysis patterns we cover is **Large-Scale Patterns**. They are about the coarse grain structure of software traces and logs where the division unit is often a component or some high-level functionality. Their pattern language names are

- Characteristic Message Block

- Background Components

- Foreground Components

- Layered Periodization

- Focus of Tracing

- Event Sequence Order ↓

- Trace Frames

Characteristic Message Block

Figure 5-1 shows a bird's eye view of Process Monitor log: a typical binary software trace generated using Dump2Picture.[1] However, we are concerned with formatted textual representations.

---

[1] www.dumpanalysis.org/dump2picture

© Dmitry Vostokov 2023
D. Vostokov, *Fundamentals of Trace and Log Analysis,*
https://doi.org/10.1007/978-1-4842-9896-1_5

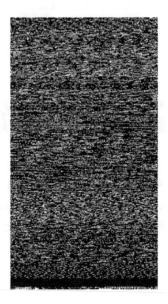

Figure 5-1. *An illustration of a typical binary software trace*

Textual representations can also be viewed from a bird's eye perspective (Figure 5-2). Irregularities in formatting make it easier to see the coarse blocked structure of a software trace or log. Typical examples here are uniform debugging message stream and some very long repeated activity like retries. Such blocks of output can be seen when scrolling trace viewer output, but if a viewer supports zooming, it is possible to get an overview and jump directly into **Characteristic Message Block**. For example, we can open a log file in a word processor, choose the smallest font possible, and select multipage view. Visual Studio Code has a similar bird's eye view and can be used for loading and searching large log files. Sometimes this pattern is useful to ignore bulk messages and start the analysis around block boundaries.

Figure 5-2. *An illustration of **Characteristic Message Block** pattern*

Background Components

To illustrate the **Background** and **Foreground Components** (also called **Modules**) analysis pattern, let's suppose we are troubleshooting a graphical user interface issue using a software trace containing the output from all components of the problem system. User interface components and their messages are foreground for a trace viewer (or a person) against numerous **background components** such as database, file, and registry access, shown in light shades of gray (Figure 5-3). So we see that the choice of Foreground and Background Components depends on a problem.

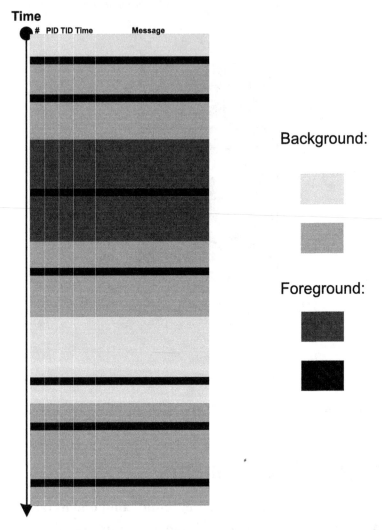

Time

PID TID Time   Message

Background:

Foreground:

Figure 5-3. *An illustration of **Background Components** pattern*

Related patterns are

- Foreground Components

Foreground Components

Trace viewers such as Process Monitor can filter out (or exclude)
Background Component messages and present only **Foreground
Components** (that we call *module* or *component foregrounding*,
Figure 5-4). Here background modules can be considered as noise to filter
out. But, of course, this process is iterative, and parts of what once was
foreground become background and candidates for further filtering.

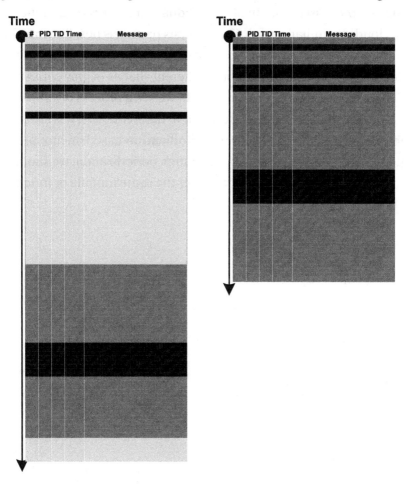

Figure 5-4. *An illustration of **Foreground Components** pattern*

Related patterns are

- Background Components

Layered Periodization

The periodization of software trace messages may include individual messages, then aggregated messages from threads, and then aggregated threads into processes and, finally, individual computers (in a client-server, cloud, or similar sense). This analysis pattern is best illustrated graphically. In Figure 5-5, first, we see a message layer on the right and then, on the left, a thread layer where different shades of gray correspond to different TIDs. Then, further on the left, we see a process layer where other different shades of gray correspond to different PIDs. It is also possible to have a different **Layered Periodization** based on modules, functions, and individual messages. For such periodization, we should remember that different threads can enter the same module or function.

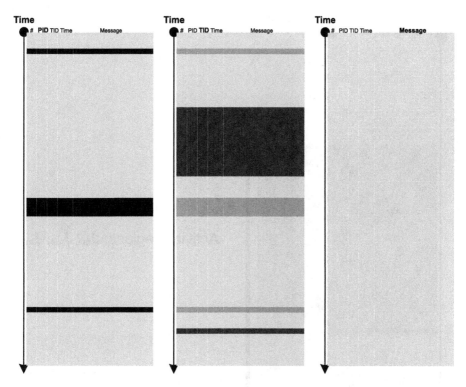

Figure 5-5. *An illustration of **Layered Periodization** pattern*

Focus of Tracing

A software trace consists of the so-called **Activity Regions** with syntactical and visual aspects of trace analysis. In contrast, the **Focus of Tracing** brings attention to the changing semantics of trace message flow, for example, from logon messages during user session initialization to database search. Figure 5-6 graphically illustrates this pattern where the tracing focus region spans three regions of activity.

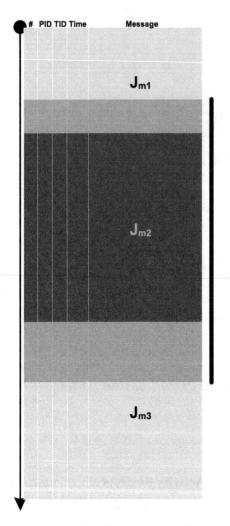

Activity Regions: J_{m1}, J_{m2}, J_{m3}

Figure 5-6. *An illustration of* ***Focus of Tracing*** *pattern*

Related patterns are

- Activity Region

Event Sequence Order

In any system, there is an expected **Event Sequence Order** as a precondition to its normal behavior. Any out-of-order events should raise the suspicion bar as they might result or lead to synchronization problems such as race conditions and deadlocks (Figure 5-7). It need not be a sequence of trace messages from different threads but also from processes; for example, process image load events can indicate a misconfiguration in process startup order.

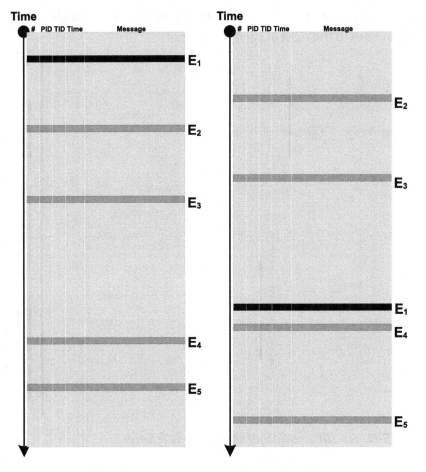

Figure 5-7. *An illustration of **Event Sequence Order** pattern*

Related patterns are

- Significant Event

- Anchor Messages

Trace Frames

Our next pattern is **Trace Frames**, and to make it more understandable, Figure 5-8 shows a good example from the Visual Studio editor where we can expand and collapse nested function declarations. I highlighted frames in lines to the right of each screenshot.

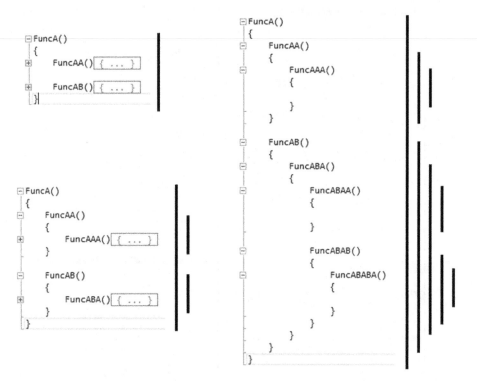

Figure 5-8. *An illustration of source code frames*

Similar to source code, we also have **Trace Frames** in software traces (Figure 5-9). Some products use indentation in textual logs. At the level of a software trace or filtered thread, or **Adjoint Thread of Activity**, we can clearly see **Discontinuities**.

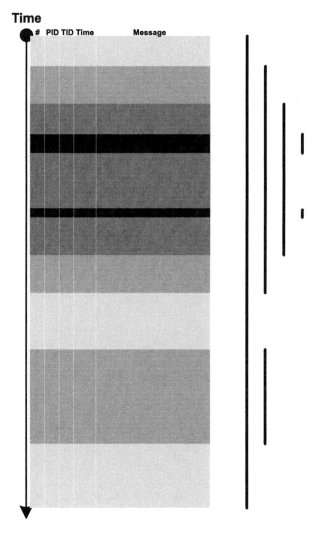

Figure 5-9. *An illustration of **Trace Frames** pattern*

Related patterns are

- Thread of Activity

- Adjoint Thread

- Truncated Trace

- Discontinuity

Summary

In this chapter, we introduced the basic trace and log analysis patterns from the **Large-Scale Patterns** category. The next chapter introduces **Activity Patterns**.

CHAPTER 6

Activity Patterns

The fifth block of patterns relates to various software activities we see in traces and logs. Most of them involve time dependency. Their pattern language names are

- Thread of Activity ↓
- Adjoint Thread of Activity ↓
- No Activity
- Activity Region
- Discontinuity ↓
- Time Delta ↓
- Glued Activity
- Break-in Activity ↓
- Resume Activity ↓

Thread of Activity

The **Thread of Activity** pattern is about trace messages associated with a particular TID. Usually, when we see an error indication or some interesting message, we select its current thread and investigate what happened in this process and thread before (Figure 6-1). Looking at threads, we can spot discontinuities that can be signs of inter-process

© Dmitry Vostokov 2023
D. Vostokov, *Fundamentals of Trace and Log Analysis*,
https://doi.org/10.1007/978-1-4842-9896-1_6

communication and even CPU activity if code loops are not covered by trace statements (the so-called **Sparse Trace** pattern). Here a supplemental memory dump may reveal stack traces (backtraces) and help in further diagnostics of abnormal software behavior.

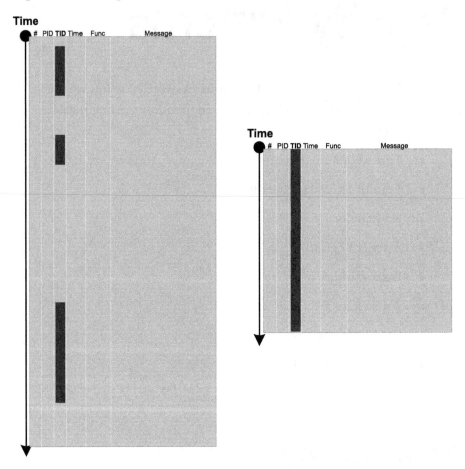

Figure 6-1. *An illustration of **Thread of Activity** pattern*

Related patterns are

- Discontinuity

- Sparse Trace

Adjoint Thread of Activity

As I mentioned in Chapter 1, the **Adjoint Thread** is an extension of the **Thread of Activity** pattern. In the picture, we see a message stream where some messages are coming from specific TID shown in the dark gray color. Suppose we are interested in some specific trace **Message Invariant**, such as related to the CreateProcess API call. In such trace messages, usually in ETW trace format, there is some message invariant part saved in short binary form, possibly in GUID format for fast recording together with some data as process image name. Later, when this message is formatted for display, any variant part is formatted and appended to it. However, because of the invariant part, it is possible to filter such messages and form an **Adjoint Thread of Activity** (Figure 6-2).

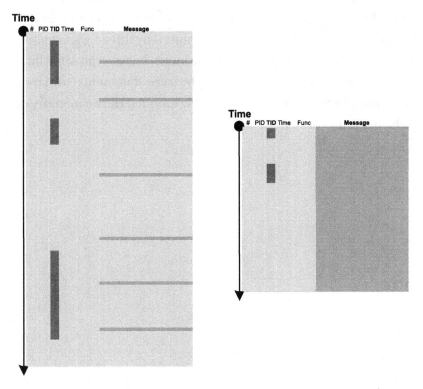

Figure 6-2. An illustration of *Adjoint Thread of Activity* pattern

Related patterns are

- Thread of Activity

- Message Invariant

No Activity

A **Discontinuity** pattern is seen when some activity ceases to manifest itself in trace messages. Its limit is **No Activity**, where the absence of activity can be seen at a thread level or a process level, or a component level, with the latter similar to the **Missing Component** pattern. The difference from the latter pattern is that we know for certain that we selected our modules for tracing but don't see any trace messages at all (Figure 6-3). If a process starts before a tracing session and there is no activity, we can think of it as hanging caused by thread wait chains, deadlocks, terminated threads, or infinite loops. It is also possible that certain parts of the code are not covered by trace statements (the so-called **Sparse Trace** pattern), and they are simply looping. Here a memory dump would be helpful.

Time

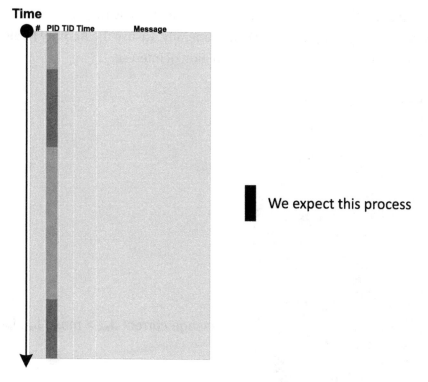

We expect this process

*Figure 6-3. An illustration of **No Activity** pattern*

Related patterns are

- Discontinuity

- Sparse Trace

- Missing Component

Activity Region

When looking at long traces with millions of messages, we can see regions of activity where **Message Current** (J_m, msg/s) is much higher than in surrounding temporal regions or partitions a trace into **Characteristic**

Message Blocks where gaps between them are filled with some background activity (Figure 6-4). But generally, we use the **Activity Region** pattern name for some trace and log region of interest.

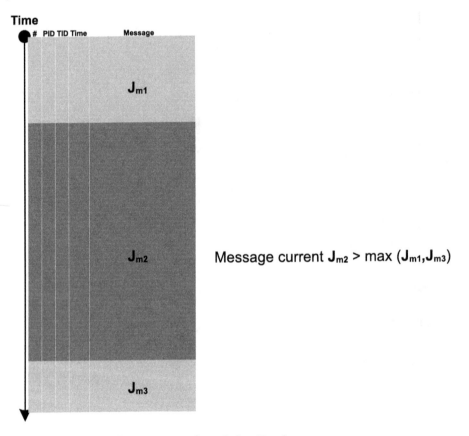

Figure 6-4. An illustration of **Activity Region** pattern

Related patterns are

- Message Current
- Characteristic Message Block

Discontinuity

Sometimes we may see delays in an application or service startup, user session initialization, process launch sequences, long response times, and simply the absence of response (Figure 6-5). All these problems can be reflected in software traces showing sudden time gaps in **Threads of Activity**. Of course, there can be different causes for **Discontinuities**, such as threads blocked in inter-process communication, but with a preselected time-out, there may be some CPU-intensive computation not covered by trace statements in source code (**Sparse Trace** pattern). It could also be the case of **Missing Components** not being selected for tracing.

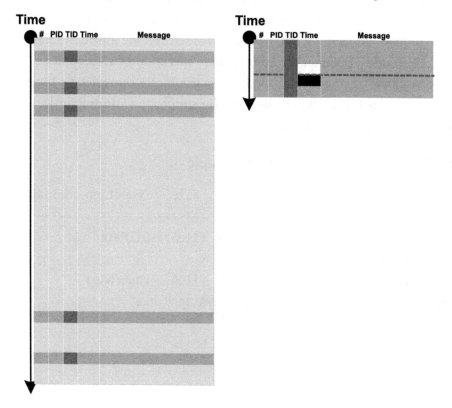

Figure 6-5. *An illustration of **Discontinuity** pattern*

Related patterns are

- Thread of Activity

- Missing Component

- Sparse Trace

Time Delta

The **Time Delta** pattern is closely related to **Discontinuity**. This analysis pattern is a time interval between **Significant Events** we are interested in or just some found delay, as the example in Listing 6-1 (see also Figure 6-5). In the trace fragment, we are interested in the dllA activity from its load until it launches appB.exe. We see that the time delta was only 10 seconds. But after the launch, there was another 30-second delay until the tracing was stopped. When troubleshooting delays, their time should be included in **Basic Facts** (or supporting information) accompanying software traces and logs.

Listing 6-1. Time Delta pattern example

```
#     Module PID  TID  Time          File    Function  Message
--------------------------------------------------------------
6060  dllA   1604 7108 10:06:21.746 fileA.c DllMain
DLL_PROCESS_ATTACH
24480 dllA   1604 7108 10:06:32.262 fileA.c LaunchApp
Exec Path: C:\Program Files\CompanyA\appB.exe
```

Related patterns are

- Basic Facts

- Thread of Activity

- Discontinuity

- Significant Event

Glued Activity

Adjoint Thread invariants that we name as ATIDs (like TIDs for threads) can be reused, giving rise to software traces where two separate execution entities (different ATIDs such as 2 and 3 in Figure 6-6) are glued together in one trace. For example, I observed PID reuse several times. But in the case of other OS and adjoint thread invariants, which can be reused, I abstracted this **Glued Activity** pattern for ATIDs. Other similar examples might include different instances of modules sharing the same name, source code, or even, in general, periodic tracing sessions appended to the end of the same trace file.

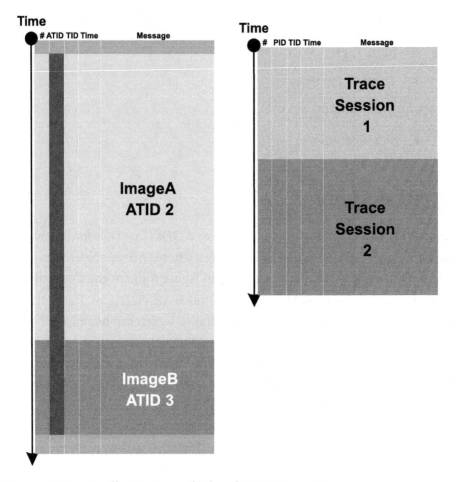

Figure 6-6. *An illustration of **Glued Activity** pattern*

Related patterns are

- Adjoint Thread of Activity

Break-in Activity

Break-in Activity analysis pattern (Figure 6-7) covers a message or a set of messages that surfaces just before the end of **Discontinuity** of **Thread of Activity** or **Adjoint Thread** and possibly triggered activity continuation (**Resume Activity** pattern we cover next).

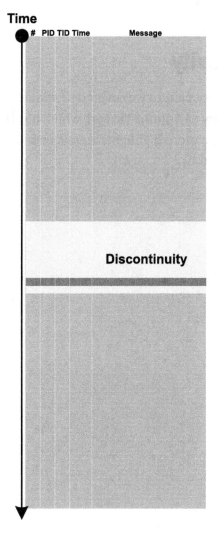

Figure 6-7. An illustration of **Break-in Activity** pattern

Related patterns are

- Thread of Activity

- Adjoint Thread of Activity

- Discontinuity

- Resume Activity

Resume Activity

If the **Break-in Activity** pattern we covered previously may be unrelated to the **Thread of Activity** or **Adjoint Thread**, which has **Discontinuity**, then the **Resume Activity** pattern highlights messages from that thread after the discontinuity (Figure 6-8).

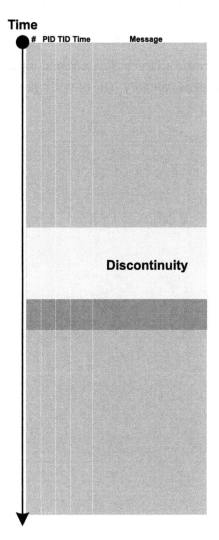

Figure 6-8. *An illustration of* ***Resume Activity*** *pattern*

Related patterns are

- Break-in Activity

- Thread of Activity

- Adjoint Thread of Activity

Summary

In this chapter, we introduced the basic trace and log analysis patterns from the **Activity Patterns** category. The next chapter introduces **Message Patterns**.

CHAPTER 7

Message Patterns

Capturing delicate moments, one gives birth to a poetry of traces...

—Ange Leccia, Motionless Journeys, by Fabien Danesi

The sixth block of patterns we cover is **Message Patterns** or patterns at the level of an individual message. Their pattern language names are

- Significant Event

- Defamiliarizing Effect

- Anchor Messages

- Diegetic Messages

- Message Change ↓

- Message Invariant

- UI Message

- Original Message

- Opposition Messages

- Implementation Discourse

- Linked Messages

- Gossip ↓

© Dmitry Vostokov 2023
D. Vostokov, *Fundamentals of Trace and Log Analysis*,
https://doi.org/10.1007/978-1-4842-9896-1_7

- Abnormal Value

- Message Context

- Marked Messages

- Incomplete History

- Message Interleave

- Fiber Bundle

Significant Event

When looking at software traces and logs and doing either a search or just scrolling, certain messages have our attention immediately (Figure 7-1). We call them **Significant Events**. It could be a recorded **Exception Stack Trace** or **Error Message**, **Basic Fact**, a trace message from **Vocabulary Index**, or just any trace message that marks the start of some activity we want to explore in depth; for example, a DLL or shared library is loaded into a process space, a process is started, or a certain function is called. The start of a trace and the end of it are trivial significant events and are used in deciding whether the trace is **Circular Trace**, and also in determining the trace recording interval (**Time Delta** pattern) or its average **Message Current**.

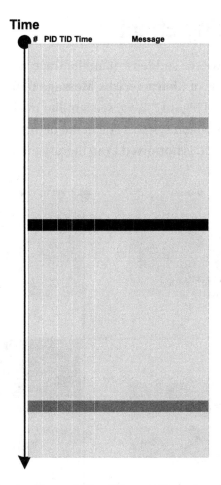

Figure 7-1. *An illustration of **Significant Event** pattern*

Related patterns are

- Exception Stack Trace

- Error Message

- Basic Facts

- Vocabulary Index

Defamiliarizing Effect

Here like in poetry, we see sudden unfamiliar trace statements across the familiar landscape of **Characteristic Message Blocks** and **Activity Regions**. On the left of Figure 7-2, we see familiar traces and, on the right, a new trace from a problem system. The name of this analysis pattern, **Defamiliarizing Effect**, is borrowed from literary theory.

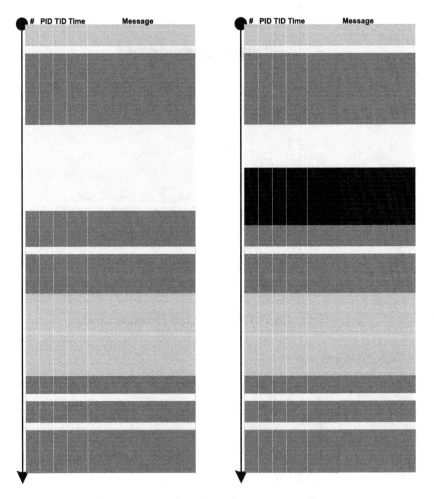

Figure 7-2. *An illustration of **Defamiliarizing Effect** pattern*

Related patterns are

- Characteristic Message Block

- Activity Region

Anchor Messages

When a software trace is very long, it is useful to partition it into several regions based on a sequence of **Anchor Messages** (Figure 7-3). The choice of them can be determined by **Vocabulary Index** or **Adjoint Thread of Activity**. For example, an ETW trace with almost 1,000,000 messages recorded during a remote desktop connection for 6 minutes can be split into 14 segments by the **Adjoint Thread** of DLL load messages. Then each region can be analyzed independently for any anomalies, for example, to answer the question of why an error handling process (wermgr.exe) was launched (Listing 7-1).

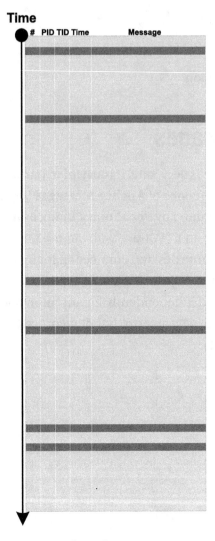

Figure 7-3. *An illustration of **Anchor Messages** pattern*

Listing 7-1. Anchor Messages pattern example

```
#        PID   TID   Time         Message
-----------------------------------------------------------------
24226    2656  3480  10:41:05.774 AppA.exe: DLL_PROCESS_ATTACH
108813   4288  4072  10:41:05.774 AppB.exe: DLL_PROCESS_ATTACH
112246   4180  3836  10:41:05.940 DllHost.exe: DLL_PROCESS_ATTACH
135473   2040  3296  10:41:12.615 AppC.exe: DLL_PROCESS_ATTACH
694723   1112  1992  10:44:23.393 AppD.exe: DLL_PROCESS_ATTACH
703962   5020  1080  10:44:42.014 DllHost.exe: DLL_PROCESS_ATTACH
705511   4680  3564  10:44:42.197 DllHost.exe: DLL_PROCESS_ATTACH
705891   1528  2592  10:44:42.307 regedit.exe: DLL_PROCESS_ATTACH
785231   2992  4912  10:45:26.516 AppE.exe: DLL_PROCESS_ATTACH
786523   3984  1156  10:45:26.605 powershell.exe: DLL_PROCESS_ATTACH
817979   4188  4336  10:45:48.707 wermgr.exe: DLL_PROCESS_ATTACH
834875   3976  1512  10:45:52.342 LogonUI.exe: DLL_PROCESS_ATTACH
835229   4116  3540  10:45:52.420 AppG.exe: DLL_PROCESS_ATTACH
```

Related patterns are

- Vocabulary Index

- Adjoint Thread of Activity

- Message Interleave

Message Interleave

Message Interleave pattern addresses several trace segmentations by interleaving regions of one set of **Anchor Messages** with another set of **Anchor Messages** (Figure 7-4). Here, in this picture, we interleave the **Adjoint Thread** of DLL load messages with the adjoint thread of DLL unload messages. Another example could be open and close messages.

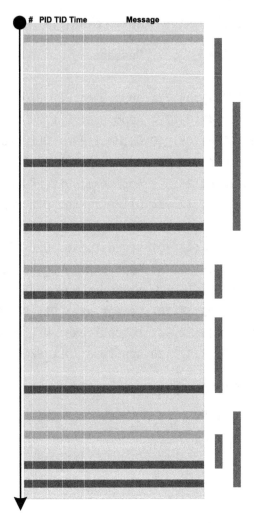

Figure 7-4. *An illustration of* **Message Interleave** *pattern*

Related patterns are

- Adjoint Thread of Activity
- Anchor Messages

Diegetic Messages

In general, we have processes or components that trace themselves and processes or components that query about other processes, components, and subsystems. In Figure 7-5, you see the difference between **Diegetic Messages** (in dark gray color) and non-diegetic trace messages (in light gray color) for PIDs. A typical example here is a user session initialization process startup sequence in a Windows remote desktop server.

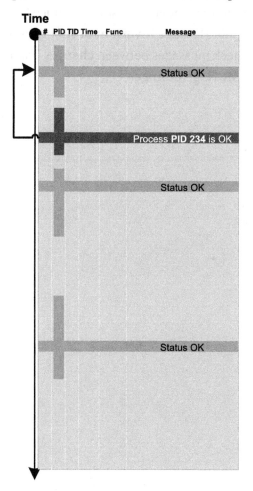

Figure 7-5. *An illustration of **Diegetic Messages** pattern*

Related patterns are

- Anchor Messages

Message Change

Often when we find **Anchor Message** related to our problem description, which has a variable part such as a status or progress report, we are interested in its evolution throughout a software trace (by creating an **Adjoint Thread** for this **Message Invariant** or simply by a search filter). And then, we can check messages between changes (Figure 7-6). Hence, we call this pattern **Message Change**.

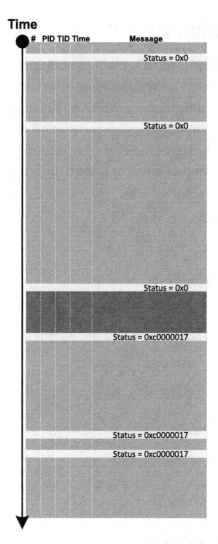

Figure 7-6. *An illustration of **Message Change** pattern*

Related patterns are

- Anchor Messages

- Message Invariant

- Adjoint Thread of Activity

Implementation Discourse

If we look at any nontrivial trace, we will see different **Implementation Discourses**. Components are written using different languages and adhere to different runtime environments, binary models, and interface frameworks. All these implementation variations influence the structure, syntax, and semantics of trace messages. For example, .NET debugging traces differ from file system driver or COM debugging or Linux strace messages. Example discourses are

- Win32 API

- MFC

- Kernel Development

- COM

- C# / .NET

- C++

- Java

- Python

- Kubernetes

- Scala/FP

Message Invariant

We have already encountered **Message Invariants** before in the context of a single software trace. Here we illustrate it for a trace set of working (normal) and nonworking (abnormal) software traces. Recall that most of the time, software trace and log messages coming from the same source code fragment (the so-called **PLOT**, Program Lines of Trace) contain invariant parts such as function and variable names, descriptions, and mutable parts such as pointer values and error codes. In a comparative analysis of several trace files, we are often interested in message differences. For example, in one troubleshooting scenario, certain objects were not created correctly for one user. We suspected a different object version was linked to a user profile. Separate application debug traces were recorded for each user, and we could see version 0x4 for the problem user and 0x5 for all other normal users (Listing 7-2).

Listing 7-2. Message Invariant pattern example

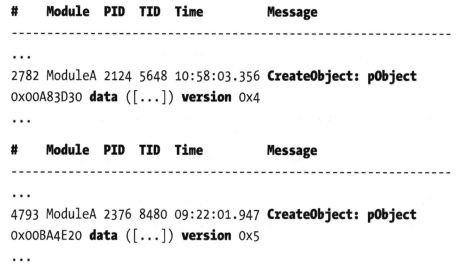

```
#    Module  PID   TID   Time           Message
-----------------------------------------------------------------
...
2782 ModuleA 2124  5648  10:58:03.356 CreateObject: pObject
0x00A83D30 data ([...]) version 0x4
...

#    Module  PID   TID   Time           Message
-----------------------------------------------------------------
...
4793 ModuleA 2376  8480  09:22:01.947 CreateObject: pObject
0x00BA4E20 data ([...]) version 0x5
...
```

Related patterns are

- Trace Set

UI Message

UI Message pattern is very useful for troubleshooting system-wide issues because we can map visual behavior to various **Activity Regions** and consider such messages as **Significant Events**. For example, by filtering by TID, we can create a **Thread of Activity**, and by filtering by module or PID, we can create an **Adjoint Thread of Activity** (Listing 7-3).

Listing 7-3. UI Message pattern example of original and filtered traces

```
#    Module  PID  TID  Time          Message
------------------------------------------------------------
...
2782 ModuleA 2124 5648 10:58:03.356 CreateWindow: Title "..."
Class "..."
...
3512 ModuleA 2124 5648 10:58:08.154 Menu command: Save Data
...
3583 ModuleA 2124 5648 10:58:08.155 CreateWindow: Title "Save
As" Class "Dialog"
[... Data update and replication related messages ...]
4483 ModuleA 2124 5648 10:58:12.342 DestroyWindow: Title "Save
As" Class "Dialog"
...

#    Module  PID  TID  Time          Message
------------------------------------------------------------
...
2782 ModuleA 2124 5648 10:58:03.356 CreateWindow: Title "..."
Class "..."
```

```
3512 ModuleA 2124 5648 10:58:08.154 Menu command: Save Data
3583 ModuleA 2124 5648 10:58:08.155 CreateWindow: Title "Save
As" Class "Dialog"
4483 ModuleA 2124 5648 10:58:12.342 DestroyWindow: Title "Save
As" Class "Dialog"
...
```

Related patterns are

- Activity Region

- Significant Event

- Thread of Activity

- Adjoint Thread of Activity

Original Message

Original Message pattern deals with software trace messages where a certain **Message Invariant** is repeated several times, but only the first message occurrence has significance for software trace analysis. One such example is shown here for library load events (Listing 7-4). We form **Adjoint Thread** and look for ".dll" messages. We are interested in the first occurrence of a specific name because, in our troubleshooting context, we need to know the time it was loaded first. This pattern is called **Original Message** and not **First Message** because, in other contexts and cases, the message wording and data might differ for the first and subsequent messages.

Listing 7-4. Original Message pattern example

```
#      Module  PID    TID    Time          Message
------------------------------------------------------------------
...
35835 ModuleA 12332 11640 18:27:28.720 LoadLibrary: \Program
Files\MyProduct\System32\MyDLL.dll PID 12332
...
37684 ModuleA 12332 9576  18:27:29.063 LoadLibrary: \Program
Files\MyProduct\System32\MyDLL.dll PID 12332
...
37687 ModuleA 12332 9576  18:27:29.064 LoadLibrary: \Program
Files\MyProduct\System32\MyDLL.dll PID 12332
...
```

Related patterns are

- Message Invariant

- Adjoint Thread of Activity

Linked Messages

Sometimes we have the so-called **Linked Messages** through some common parameter or attribute. One such example is illustrated in Listing 7-5 and Figure 7-7, and it is related to kernel process creation notifications. Here we got **Adjoint Thread** for a module that intercepts such events (not shown on the trace example for visual clarity). We see messages linked through PID and PPID (parent PID) parameter relationship.

Listing 7-5. Linked Messages pattern example

```
#       PID  Message
-----------------------------------------------
...
128762 1260 CreateProcess: PPID 1260 PID 6356
...
128785 6356 ImageLoad: AppA.exe PID 6356
...
131137 6356 CreateProcess: PPID 6356 PID 6280
...
131239 6280 ImageLoad: AppB.exe PID 6280
...
132899 6356 CreateProcess: PPID 6356 PID 8144
...
132906 8144 ImageLoad: AppC.exe PID 8144
...
```

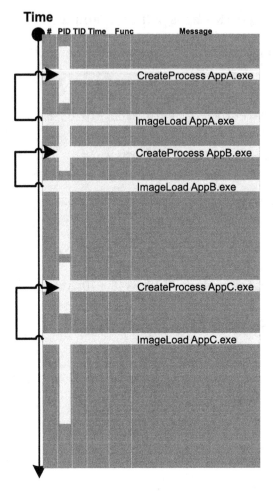

Figure 7-7. *An illustration of **Linked Messages** pattern*

Related patterns are

- Adjoint Thread of Activity

Gossip

This pattern has a funny name. It is called **Gossip** instead of **Duplicated Message** to allow the possibility of syntax and semantics of the same message to be distorted in subsequent trace messages from different **Adjoint Threads**. In Listing 7-6, in the first top example, you see a distortion-free example of the same message content seen in different modules. To make analysis easier, when using **Event Sequence Order** or **Message Interleave** analysis patterns, it is recommended to choose messages from one source instead of mixing events from different sources, as in the second bottom example in Listing 7-6.

Listing 7-6. Gossip pattern example

```
#     Module  PID  TID  Message
...
26875 ModuleA 2172 5284 LoadImage: \Device\HarddiskVolume2\
Windows\System32\notepad.exe PID 0x000000000000087C
26876 ModuleB 2172 5284 LoadImage: \Device\HarddiskVolume2\
Windows\System32\notepad.exe, PID (2172)
26877 ModuleC 2172 5284 ImageLoad: fileName=notepad.exe, pid:
000000000000087C

...

#     Module  PID  TID  Message
...
26875 ModuleA 2172 5284 LoadImage: \Device\HarddiskVolume2\
Windows\System32\notepad.exe PID 0x000000000000087C

...

33132 ModuleA 4180 2130 LoadImage: \Device\HarddiskVolume2\
Windows\System32\calc.exe PID 0x0000000000001054

...
```

Related patterns are

- Adjoint Thread of Activity

- Event Sequence Order

- Message Interleave

Abnormal Value

The **Abnormal Value** pattern is about abnormal or unexpected values in a software trace or log (Figure 7-8).

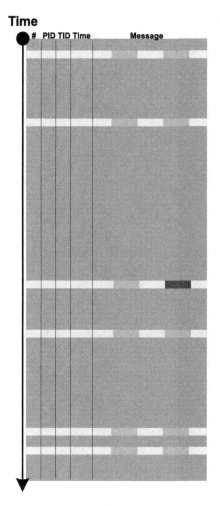

Figure 7-8. *An illustration of **Abnormal Value** pattern*

Message Context

Most of the time, we analyze not in the isolated messages but in a surrounding **Message Context**, which is a set of messages having some relation to the chosen message and usually found in the message stream in some close proximity (Figure 7-9).

95

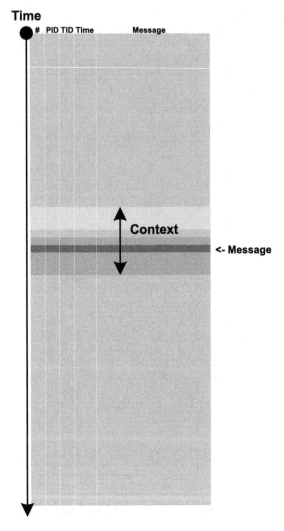

Figure 7-9. *An illustration of **Message Context** pattern*

Related patterns are

- Significant Event

- Anchor Message

Marked Messages

The **Marked Messages** pattern groups trace messages based on having some feature or property. For example, marked messages may point to some domain of software activity such as related to functional requirements and, therefore, may help in troubleshooting and debugging. Unmarked messages include all other messages that don't say anything about such activities (although they may include messages pointing to such activities indirectly that we are unaware of) or messages that say explicitly that no such activity has occurred. We can annotate any trace or log after analysis, as in Listing 7-7, to compare it with the **Master Trace** pattern (which is a normally expected trace corresponding to functional requirements). Sometimes, a non-present activity can be a marked activity corresponding to all-inclusive unmarked present activity (e.g., the **No Activity** pattern).

Listing 7-7. Marked Messages pattern example where [+] activity is present in a trace and [-] activity is undetected or not present

```
session database queries [+]
session initialization [-]
socket activity [+]
process A launched [+]
process B launched [-]
process A exited [-]
```

Related patterns are

- Master Trace

- No Activity

Fiber Bundle

Modern software trace recording, visualization, and analysis tools such as Process Monitor provide stack traces associated with trace messages. We can consider stack traces as software traces as well and, in a more general case, bundle them together (or attach them as fibers) to a base software trace or log. For example, a trace message that mentions an IRP (a structure passed to drivers) can have its I/O stack attached together with a thread stack trace with function calls leading to a function that emits the trace message (Figure 7-10). The **Fiber Bundle** pattern differs from **Exception Stack Trace**, which is just a reported stack trace formatted as trace messages in software trace or log.

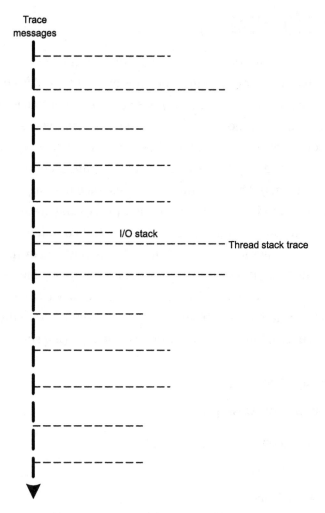

Figure 7-10. *An illustration of **Fiber Bundle** pattern*

Related patterns are

- Exception Stack Trace

Incomplete History

A large part of a typical software trace consists of requests and responses, for example, function or object method calls and returns. The code that generates trace messages is called *response-complete* if it traces both requests and responses. For such code (except in cases where tracing is stopped before a response, **Truncated Trace**), the absence of expected responses could be a sign of blocked threads or quiet exception processing (handled exceptions). The code that generates trace messages is called *exception-complete* if it also traces exception processing. *Response-complete* and *exception-complete* code is called *call-complete*. If we don't see response messages for *call-complete* code, we have **Incomplete History**, and this might be because of either execution problems or **Sparse Trace** (i.e., code is not covered by tracing). In general, we can talk about the absence of certain messages in a trace as a deviation from the standard trace sequence template corresponding to a use case (the so-called **Master Trace** pattern).

Related patterns are

- Opposition Messages

- Sparse Trace

- Truncated Trace

- Master Trace

Opposition Messages

Opposition Messages pattern covers the pairs of opposite messages usually found in software traces and logs, such as the list in Listing 7-8. The absence of an opposite may point to some problems, such as synchronization and leaks or Incomplete History (such as wait chains). Of course, there can always be a possibility that a second term is missing due to **Sparse Trace** not being covered by sufficient trace statements in the source code, but this is a poor implementation choice that leads to much confusion during troubleshooting and debugging.

Listing 7-8. Opposition Messages examples

```
open - close
create – destroy (discard)
allocate - free (deallocate)
call - return
enter - exit (leave)
load - unload
save - load
lock - unlock
map - unmap
```

Related patterns are

- Incomplete History

- Sparse Trace

Summary

In this chapter, we introduced the basic trace and log analysis patterns from the **Message Patterns** category. The next chapter introduces **Block Patterns**.

CHAPTER 8

Block Patterns

The seventh type of patterns we cover is **Block patterns** of message aggregates, message blocks, and correlation inside the same trace or log. Their pattern language names are

- Macrofunction

- Periodic Message Block

- Intra-correlation

Macrofunction

Several trace messages may form a single semantic unit that we call **Macrofunction** compared to individual trace messages that serve the role of "microfunctions." In Listing 8-1, we provide an example of a software log fragment for an attempt to update a database. We can consider **Macrofunction** as a use case. It involves different PIDs for a client and a server. So we see these **Macrofunctions** need not be from the same ATID (**Adjoint Thread** TID).

© Dmitry Vostokov 2023
D. Vostokov, *Fundamentals of Trace and Log Analysis*,
https://doi.org/10.1007/978-1-4842-9896-1_8

Listing 8-1. Macrofunction pattern example

```
#     Module  PID  TID   Time          Message
----------------------------------------------------------------
...
42582 DBClient 5492 9476  11:04:33.398 Opening connection
...
42585 DBClient 5492 9476  11:04:33.398 Sending SQL command
...
42589 DBServer 6480 10288 11:04:33.399 Executing SQL command
...
42592 DBClient 5492 9476  11:04:33.400 Closing connection
...
```

Periodic Message Block

The **Periodic Message Block** pattern (Figure 8-1) is similar to the
Periodic Error pattern but not limited to errors or failure status reports,
for example, when some **Adjoint Thread** (such as messages from specific
PID) stop to appear after the middle of the trace and, after that, there are
repeated blocks of **Message Invariants** from different PIDs with their
threads checking for some condition (such as waiting for an event) and
reporting time-outs. There can also be **Discontinuities** between the same
message blocks from **Periodic Message Blocks**.

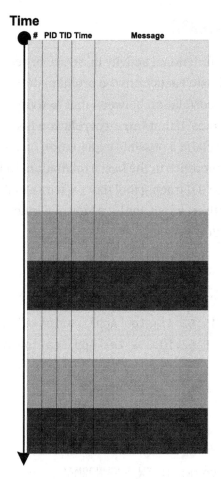

Figure 8-1. *An illustration of **Periodic Message Block** pattern*

Related patterns are

- Periodic Error

- Adjoint Thread of Activity

- Invariant Message

- Discontinuity

Intra-correlation

Sometimes we see a functional activity in a trace or see some messages that correspond to **Basic Facts** from the problem description. Then we might want to find a correlation between that **Activity Region** or facts and another part of the trace. If that **Intra-correlation** fits into our problem description, we may claim a possible explanation or, if we are lucky, we have just found an inference to the best explanation. In Listing 8-2, there is an example of one GUI tracing tool that we wrote in the past. We can see that most of the time, when `Application A` window loses focus, `Application B` window gets it.

Listing 8-2. Intra-correlation pattern example

```
Handle: 00050586 Class: "Application A Class" Title: ""
Title changed at 15:52:4:3 to "Application A"
Title changed at 15:52:10:212 to "Application A - File1"
...
Process ID: 89c
Thread ID: d6c
...
Visible: true
Window placement command: SW_SHOWNORMAL
Placement changed at 15:54:57:506 to SW_SHOWMINIMIZED
Placement changed at 15:55:2:139 to SW_SHOWNORMAL
Foreground: false
Foreground changed at 15:52:4:3 to true
Foreground changed at 15:53:4:625 to false
Foreground changed at 15:53:42:564 to true
Foreground changed at 15:53:44:498 to false
Foreground changed at 15:53:44:498 to true
Foreground changed at 15:53:44:592 to false
```

```
Foreground changed at 15:53:45:887 to true
Foreground changed at 15:53:47:244 to false
Foreground changed at 15:53:47:244 to true
Foreground changed at 15:53:47:353 to false
Foreground changed at 15:54:26:416 to true
Foreground changed at 15:54:27:55 to false
Foreground changed at 15:54:27:55 to true
Foreground changed at 15:54:27:180 to false
...

Handle: 000D0540 Class: "App B" Title: "Application B"
...
Process ID: 3ac
Thread ID: bd4
...
Foreground: false
Foreground changed at 15:50:36:972 to true
Foreground changed at 15:50:53:732 to false
Foreground changed at 15:50:53:732 to true
Foreground changed at 15:50:53:826 to false
Foreground changed at 15:51:51:352 to true
Foreground changed at 15:51:53:941 to false
```
Foreground changed at 15:53:8:135 to true
```
Foreground changed at 15:53:8:182 to false
Foreground changed at 15:53:10:178 to true
Foreground changed at 15:53:13:938 to false
Foreground changed at 15:53:30:443 to true
Foreground changed at 15:53:31:20 to false
Foreground changed at 15:53:31:20 to true
...
```

Related patterns are

- Basic Facts
- Activity Regions

Summary

In this chapter, we introduced the basic trace and log analysis patterns from the **Block Patterns** category. The next chapter introduces **Trace Set Patterns**.

CHAPTER 9

Trace Set Patterns

The eighth block of patterns we cover is patterns for **Trace Sets** when we have several software traces and logs. Their pattern language names are

- Master Trace

- Bifurcation Point

- Inter-correlation

- Relative Density

- News Value

- Impossible Trace

- Split Trace

Master Trace

When reading and analyzing software traces and logs, we always compare them to **Master Trace**, a standard software trace corresponding to the functional use case (Figure 9-1). When looking at the software trace from a system, we either know the correct sequence of **Activity Regions**, expect certain **Background** and **Foreground Components**, and certain **Event Sequence Order**, or mentally construct a model based on our experience and **Implementation Discourse**. Software engineers usually internalize software master traces when they construct code and write

© Dmitry Vostokov 2023
D. Vostokov, *Fundamentals of Trace and Log Analysis*,
https://doi.org/10.1007/978-1-4842-9896-1_9

tracing code for supportability. For other people supporting a product during a post-construction phase, it is important to have a repository of traces corresponding to **Master Traces**. Such repositories help in finding deviations after **Bifurcation Point**, for example. For a product that is meant to run on various systems, working scenario traces can correspond to **Master Traces**.

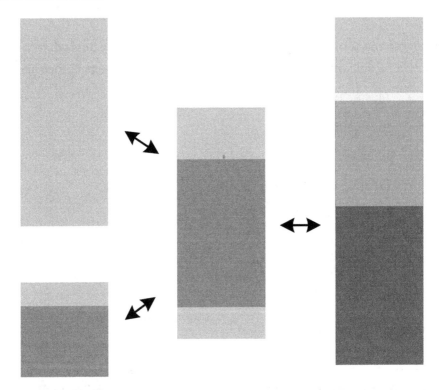

Figure 9-1. *An illustration of **Master Trace** pattern*

Related patterns are

- Activity Regions

- Background Components

- Foreground Components

- Event Sequence Order

- Guest Component

- Implementation Discourse

- Bifurcation Point

Bifurcation Point

This pattern name is borrowed from catastrophe theory.[1] It means a trace message, after which software traces diverge for working and nonworking abnormal scenarios. One such abstracted example is illustrated in Figure 9-2. In Listing 9-1, we have a software trace from a normal working environment, and in Listing 9-2, we have a software trace from a problem nonworking environment. We see that messages A, B, C, and further are identical up to the Query result message. However, the last message differs greatly in reported results X and Y. After that, the message distribution differs greatly in both size and content. Despite the same tracing time, say 15 seconds, **Message Current** is 155 msg/s for working and 388 msg/s for the nonworking case. **Bifurcation Points** are easily observed when the tracing noise ratio is small and, in the case of full traces, could be achieved by filtering irrelevant **Background Components**.

Listing 9-1. A software trace example from a normal working environment

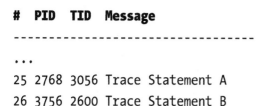

```
#   PID   TID   Message
------------------------------------
...
25 2768 3056 Trace Statement A
26 3756 2600 Trace Statement B
```

---

[1] https://en.wikipedia.org/wiki/Catastrophe_theory

```
27 3756 2600 Trace Statement C
...
149 3756 836 Query result: X
150 3756 836 Trace Statement 150.1
151 3756 836 Trace Statement 151.1
152 3756 836 Trace Statement 152.1
153 3756 836 Trace Statement 153.1
...
```

Listing 9-2. A software trace example from a problem nonworking environment

```
#  PID   TID  Message
-----------------------------------
...
27 2768 3056 Trace Statement A
28 3756 2176 Trace Statement B
29 3756 2176 Trace Statement C
...
151 3756 5940 Query result: Y
152 3756 5940 Trace Statement 152.2
153 3756 5940 Trace Statement 153.2
154 3756 5940 Trace Statement 154.2
155 3756 5940 Trace Statement 155.2
...
```

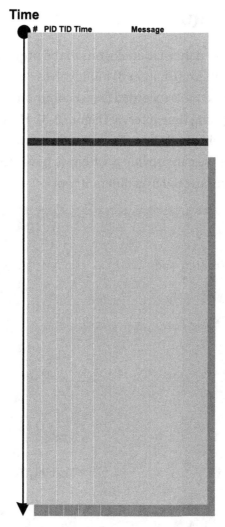

Figure 9-2. *An illustration of **Bifurcation Point** pattern*

Inter-correlation

The **Inter-correlation** pattern is analogous to the previously described **Intra-correlation** pattern (Chapter 8) but involves several traces from possibly different trace tools recorded (most commonly) at the same time or during an overlapping time interval (Figure 9-3). However, the purpose of using different tracing tools is to cover system events more completely. One of the examples we can provide is when we have **Discontinuity**, and its interval events are covered by a different tool.

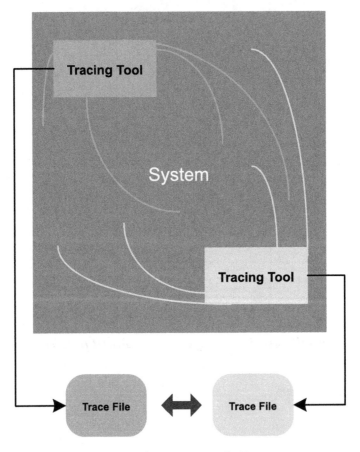

Figure 9-3. *An illustration of **Inter-correlation** pattern*

Related patterns are

- Intra-correlation

- Basic Facts

- Discontinuity

- Sparse Trace

Relative Density

The **Relative Density** analysis pattern describes anomalies related to the semantically related pairs of trace messages, for example, "data arrival" and "data display." Their **Message Densities** can be put in a ratio and compared between working and nonworking scenarios. Recall that **Message Density** is the ratio of the number of specific messages to the total number of messages in a software trace. Because the total number of trace messages cancels each other, we have a mutual ratio of the two message types. One hypothetical example is shown in Figure 9-4. In the left picture, we see the ratio of "data arrival" to "data display" is 1/1. In the right picture, we see the increased ratio of "data arrival" to "data display" messages (3/1), and this accounts for reported visual data loss and sluggish GUI.

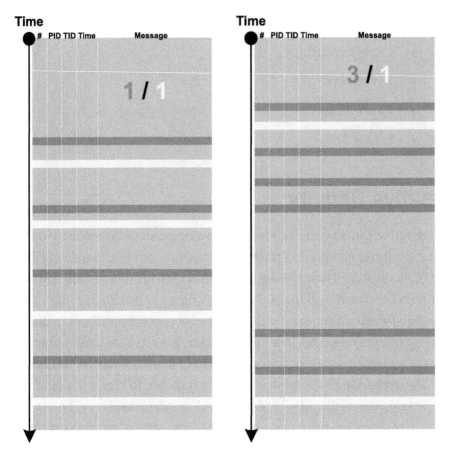

Figure 9-4. *An illustration of **Relative Density** pattern*

Related patterns are

- Message Density

News Value

The **News Value** analysis pattern assigns relative importance to software traces for problem-solving purposes, especially when related to problem description (**Basic Facts**), recent incidents, and timestamps of other supporting artifacts such as memory dumps. Assessing value is often done in conjunction with trace **Inter-correlation** analysis of the most recent logs. For example, in Figure 9-5, in relation to a trace on the left (first), only the third trace has some value, as the other two were recorded either earlier or later.

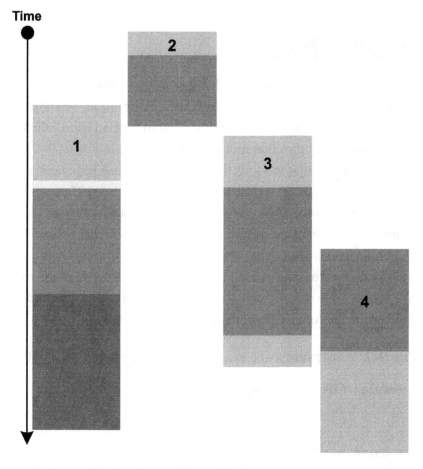

Figure 9-5. *An illustration of **News Value** pattern*

Related patterns are

- Inter-correlation

- Basic Facts

- Master Trace

Impossible Trace

Although rarely (at least for myself), it happens that when we look at a trace and then say it's an **Impossible Trace**. For example, we see in the trace fragment in Listing 9-3 that the function foo had been called. However, if we look at the corresponding source code in Listing 9-4, we will see that something is missing: the function bar must have been called with its own set of trace messages we don't see in the trace. Here we might suspect that the runtime code was being modified, perhaps by patching. In other cases of missing messages, we can also suspect thrown exceptions or local buffer overflows that led to the wrong return address skipping the code with expected tracing statements. The mismatch between the trace and the source code we are looking at is also possible if the old source code didn't have the bar function called (**Sparse Trace** pattern).

Listing 9-3. A software trace example for Impossible Trace pattern

```
#    Module  PID TID Message
-------------------------------
...
1001 ModuleA 202 404 foo: start
1002 ModuleA 202 404 foo: end
...
```

Listing 9-4. A source code example for Impossible Trace pattern

```
void foo()
{
  TRACE("foo: start");
  bar();
  TRACE("foo: end");
}
void bar()
{
  TRACE("bar: start");
  // some code ...
  TRACE("bar: end");
}
```

Related patterns are

- Sparse Trace

Split Trace

Some tracing tools have the option to split software traces and logs into several files during long recording (Figure 9-6). Although this should be done judiciously, it is really necessary sometimes. So, what should we do if we get several large trace files, but our favorite tool can open only one trace at a time? If we know the problem happened just before the tracing session was stopped, we can look at the last such file from the file sequence. If we have small files, then we should recommend **Circular Trace**. If we need adjoint threading, another method is exporting **Split Trace** into CSV files and importing it into a tool that can load multiple files.

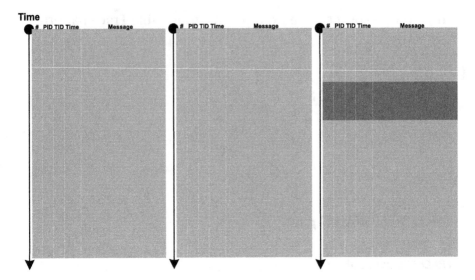

Figure 9-6. *An illustration of **Split Trace** pattern*

Related patterns are

- Circular Trace

Summary

In this chapter, we introduced the basic trace and log analysis patterns from the **Trace Set Patterns** category. The next chapter introduces **Data Patterns**.

CHAPTER 10

Data Patterns

The last block of patterns we cover is patterns for interpreting software traces and logs as data. Their pattern language names are

- Data Flow ↓

- Back Trace ↓

- Counter Value

- Data Association

- Data Selector

- Null Reference

- Signal

- Visitor Trace

- Watch Thread

- State Dump

Data Flow

If trace messages contain some character or formatted data passed from module to module or between threads and processes, it is possible to trace that data and form a **Data Flow** thread similar to the **Adjoint Thread of Activity** we have when we filter by a specific **Message Invariant**. However,

© Dmitry Vostokov 2023
D. Vostokov, *Fundamentals of Trace and Log Analysis*,
https://doi.org/10.1007/978-1-4842-9896-1_10

for **Data Flow**, we may have completely different message types. Here I illustrate **Data Flow** by a hypothetical driver communication case where the same IRP (I/O request packet) is passed between devices (Listing 10-1 and Figure 10-1). Please note that by **Data Flow**, we mean any data, which can be just an error or exception propagating through.

Listing 10-1. A software trace example for Data Flow pattern

```
...
DriverA: Device 0xA IRP 0xB
...
DriverB: Device 0xC IRP 0xB
...
DriverC: Device 0xD IRP 0xB
DriverC: Processing IRP 0xB

...
```

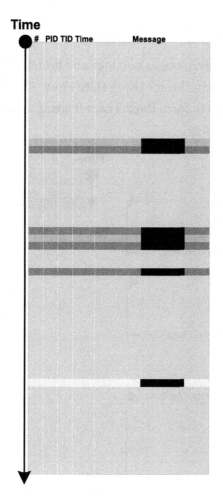

Figure 10-1. *An illustration of **Data Flow** pattern*

Related patterns are

- Adjoint Thread of Activity
- Message Invariant

Back Trace

Usually, when we analyze traces and logs and find **Anchor Message** or **Error Message**, we backtrack using **Data Flow**. Then we select the appropriate messages to form **Back Trace** leading to a possible root cause message (Figure 10-2).

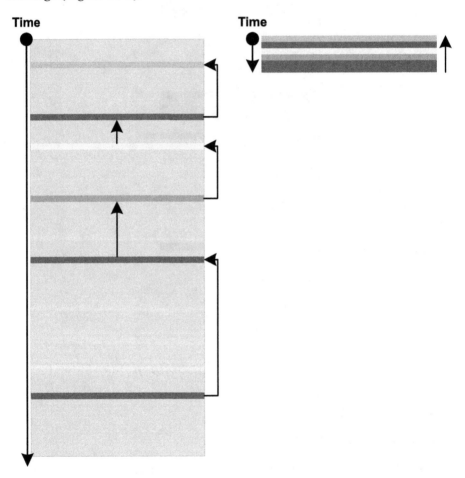

Figure 10-2. *An illustration of **Back Trace** pattern*

Counter Value

This pattern covers performance monitoring and its logs. A **Counter Value** is some variable in memory that is updated periodically to reflect some aspect of the state, for example, a performance metric. It can also be a derivative variable calculated from other different variables and presented in trace messages, for example, a more complex telemetry metric. Listing 10-2 provides an example of profile messages from Process Monitor (edited a bit for space). Profile events might be filtered off by default. The sequence of profile events is a software trace itself, so all other trace analysis patterns such as **Adjoint Thread** (different colors on graphs), **Focus of Tracing**, **Characteristic Message Block** (for graphs), **Activity Region**, **Significant Event**, and others can be applied here. Besides that, there are also **Performance**-specific patterns, such as **Global Monotonicity** and **Constant Value**, but they are beyond the scope of this book.

Listing 10-2. Counter Value pattern example

```
18:04:06 Explorer.EXE 3280 User Time: 8.4864544 seconds, Kernel
Time: 9.5004609 seconds, Private Bytes: 42,311,680, Working
Set: 10,530,816
```

Related patterns are

- Adjoint Thread of Activity

- Significant Event

- Activity Region

- Focus of Tracing

- Characteristic Message Block

Data Association

Sometimes we are interested in changes in particular {property, value} pairs or tuples $\{x_1, x_2, x_3, ...\}$ in general where x_i can be a number or a substring. It is a more general pattern than **Message Change** because such tuples can be from different sources and belong to different messages (Figure 10-3). This pattern is also different from **Data Flow**, where a value stays constant across different sources and messages. It is also different from **Gossip** pattern that involves more semantic changes. Metaphorically we can think of this pattern as a partial derivative.

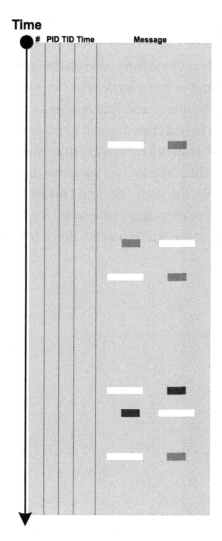

Figure 10-3. *An illustration of **Data Association** pattern*

Data Selector

Data Selector is a variant of the **Inter-correlation** trace analysis pattern where we use data found in one trace to select messages or **Adjoint Thread of Activity** in another trace. This analysis activity is depicted in Figure 10-4, where we have a client log and a corresponding server log. In the server log, we have entries for many client sessions. To select messages corresponding to our client session, we use some data attributes in the client trace, for example, the username and **Linked Messages** analysis pattern to find one of the messages in the server log that contains the same username. Then we find out which user session it belongs to and form its **Adjoint Thread**.

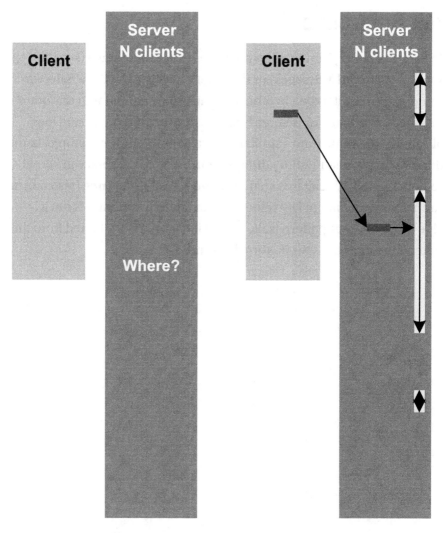

Figure 10-4. *An illustration of **Data Selector** pattern*

Null Reference

Message data may point to other messages in the same trace (see the example of **Linked Messages**) or the other trace (see the **Data Selector** example). But similar data in other messages may not point to any other messages in the same or different, perhaps **Truncated** traces and logs collected at the same time – similar to invalid pointers, for example, kernel addresses in process memory dumps, or user space addresses in kernel memory dumps. We call this analysis pattern **Null Reference** (also notice the analogy with foreign key values in data tables where Null is not a value). This analysis pattern is illustrated in Figure 10-5 adapted from the **Linked Messages** analysis pattern diagram.

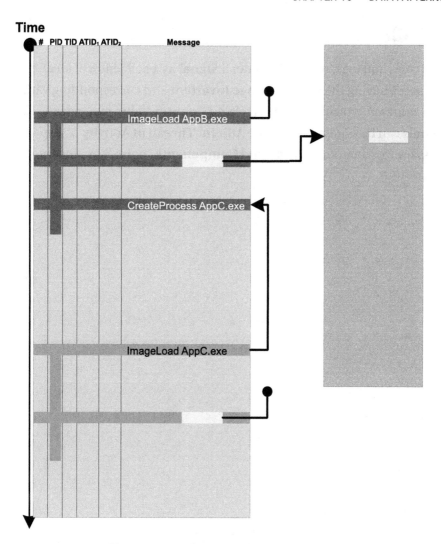

Figure 10-5. *An illustration of **Null Reference** pattern*

Signal

For traces and logs, we can consider a **Signal** as a collection of local messages having the same **Message Invariant** and corresponding variable data values. A typical example is related **Counter Value** messages. **Signals** can be obtained from the **Adjoint Thread of Activity** of a specific message (to filter out **Background Components** "noise") as illustrated in Figure 10-6.

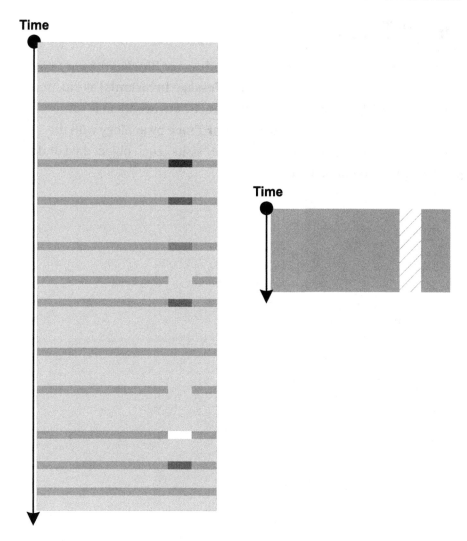

Figure 10-6. *An illustration of **Signal** pattern*

Visitor Trace

Some traces and logs may have **Periodic Message Blocks** with very similar message structure and content (mostly **Message Invariants**) as illustrated in Figure 10-7. The only significant difference between them is some unique data. We call such a pattern **Visitor Trace** by analogy with the Visitor design pattern[1] where tracing code "visits" each object data or data part to log its content or status.

---

[1] https://en.wikipedia.org/wiki/Visitor_pattern

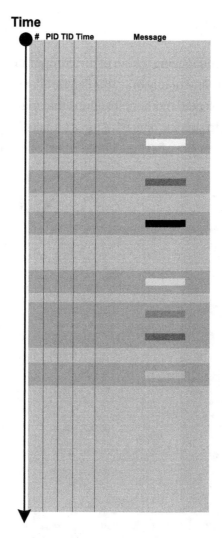

Figure 10-7. *An illustration of **Visitor Trace** pattern*

Watch Thread

When we do tracing and logging, much of the computational activity is not visible. For live tracing and debugging, this can be alleviated by adding **Watch Threads**. These are selected memory locations that may or may not be formatted according to specific data structures and are inspected at each main trace message occurrence or after specific intervals or events (Figure 10-8).

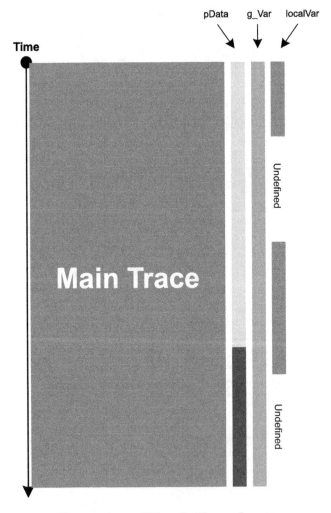

Figure 10-8. *An illustration of **Watch Thread** pattern*

State Dump

State Dump pattern solves the problem of program state analysis when memory dump generation is not available or does not help or is complicated as in the case of interpreted code. A developer identifies a set of state variables and periodically prints their values to the output logging stream (Figure 10-9). Such output may also include but is not limited to **Counter Values**.

Figure 10-9. *An illustration of State Dump pattern*

Summary

In this chapter, we introduced the basic trace and log analysis patterns from the **Data Patterns** category.

Index

A

Abnormal value, 76, 94–95
Activity patterns
    activity region, 66, 67
    adjoint thread, 63, 64
    break-in, 71, 72
    characteristic message
        blocks, 65
    discontinuity, 67, 68
    glued, 70, 71
    message invariant, 63
    no activity, 65, 66
    pattern language, 61
    sparse trace, 64
    thread, 62, 63
    time delta, 68
Activity region, 18, 25, 26, 35–38,
        55, 56, 61, 65–66, 78, 79, 88,
        89, 106, 108–110, 125
Adjoint threads
    activity patterns, 63, 64
    break-in activity, 71, 72
    data flow, 121–123
    error patterns, 22
    file/function, 8
    frames, 59

linked messages, 90–92
message patterns, 81, 82, 84
original/filtered traces, 88
partition pattern, 30
process monitor, 3, 5, 6
periodic block, 104
resume activity pattern, 72, 73
trace acceleration, 37
vocabulary pattern, 16
Adjoint thread TID (ATID), 69, 103
Anchor messages, 43, 44, 58, 75,
        79–82, 84, 85

B

Background components, 49,
        51–54, 110, 111, 132
Back trace, 121, 124
Basic facts pattern, 15, 18, 68, 69,
        77, 106, 108, 115, 116, 118
Bifurcation point, 111–113
Block patterns
    intra-correlation, 106–108
    macrofunction, 103–104
    periodic message, 104, 105
Break-in activity, 61, 71–73

© Dmitry Vostokov 2023
D. Vostokov, *Fundamentals of Trace and Log Analysis,*
https://doi.org/10.1007/978-1-4842-9896-1

Printed in the United States
by Baker & Taylor Publisher Services